MARINE WIFE,
Lyn

by

Major Ralph Stoney Bates, USMC (Ret)

DORRANCE
PUBLISHING CO
EST. 1920
PITTSBURGH, PENNSYLVANIA 15238

Dorrance Publishing Co
585 Alpha Drive
Suite 103
Pittsburgh, PA 15238
Visit our website at www.dorrancebookstore.com

ISBN: 979-8-88925-231-3
eISBN: 979-8-88925-731-8

Originally, this was to be my late wife's eulogy, but she wanted no burial, no gathering, and no funeral. She asked only to be cremated and brought home. I told her it would be; however, I said, "I'd like to write about you."

With an impish smile she responded, "How are you going to do that without me?"

My reply was, "I'll just try." This book is my try at *Marine Wife, Lyn: Straightforward, Uncomplicated, Normal, and Ordinary; Yet, Somehow, She was Extraordinarily Exceptional.*

FOREWORD

Since there's been a Marine Corps, a Navy, or any other naval or military establishment, foreign or domestic, there's been a wife (spouse) to many a man (or woman), to form a team serving the military and naval services. Many times, it is a marriage "made in heaven." However, sometimes those marriages are short-lived due to many factors related to life in the armed forces. Take mine for an example. When we married, I was a Marine Corps Drill Instructor at Parris Island. The nature of that particular duty created situations between spouses that oftentimes disrupted marital bliss, and separation, even divorce became the route out of that turmoil. Not always, but then, in those times, at Parris Island, it was not uncommon. It may have changed over these last few decades, but I kind of doubt it.

So too does deployment to unaccompanied (single, alone) foreign duty, especially combat duty oftentimes lends itself to strained relationships between the one who has waited and the one who deployed. Not uncommon were separations and/or divorce following (or before) the service person returning from foreign duty, especially war, and again joining the one who waited. Sometimes one, or both had changed. They did not have the same attitudes, aptitudes, nor personalities as before. Serving in combat sometimes changes not just the person serving, but the person waiting. They can become two very different people.

What makes the difference? Does one know who has the temperament and deportment to become a copy of the Biblical "Ruth" of *"Wherever you go, I will go. Your people shall be my people. Your God, my God,"* and the one who is not? Is it just based on the luck of the draw? Or, are there early signs pointing toward that preverbal "rocky road," or "smooth sailing" ahead?

I don't have the answer. And I am not sure anyone does. What I am sure of is that I have had a life of ups and downs, success and failure, good and bad times, peaks and valleys, that has shaped me into the eighty-five-year-old man I am at this writing, and accompanying me through this life for the past sixty-three, actually almost sixty-four-years has been the most extraordinary person I have ever known, who guided me through the bad, and showered me with the good—deserved or not! Most of the revelations regarding my bride, I've learned by piece-work, revealed in bits and pieces, gleaned through the years. However, when looking back, there were tell-tale signs early-on that clearly suggested I married up. I married above my pay grade and stayed in that position. In thought, word, and deed, she always exceeded me. Indeed, much of my admiration for her I have learned as she has been slowly dying of cancer over the last eighteen months. Now, as I promised, I must write about this person, my Lyn, my Marine wife. As a reader, you'll learn about overcoming trials and tribulations which would normally make the strong weak and the certain to become doubtful; yet, for this person I will be describing in bits and pieces, it did exactly the opposite. She didn't set the world ablaze with one or two grandiose accomplishments, but she lit a thousand fuses creating an unbroken chain of minor events to be envied by anyone fortunate enough to follow in her trace. Why? How? The reader is to determine. The answer is in the following texts. The source died as I sat beside her at 1320 (1:20 p.m.) on 12 September 2022.

Ralph Stoney Bates, Sr.
Marine/Husband/Widower

Lyn and me

May God grant me the wisdom, courage, recall, and steadfastness to honestly describe my Marine Wife, Lyn in a manner deserving of her and all military wives (spouses) throughout history that have contributed to the bulwark of the Armed Forces of the United States of America. Amen!

. . .

Final Voyage of Linda "Lyn" Gale Bates

OBITUARY PUBLISHED IN
CHARLESTON POST AND COURIER NEWSPAPER

On 12 September 2022, at 1320, my Marine Wife of almost sixty-three years, made her final voyage as I sat beside her. Together, we had created a family, a daughter, Deborah who works and resides in multiple states , a son, Stoney Jr., whereabouts unknown, and a daughter, Karen, who resides at the Home of Guiding Hands in California. Through the years together she was my rock and she lit the lamp to guide us through life together. Our life in the Marine Corps was, in a word, spectacular. We had resided and flourished at Parris Island (twice), Naval Air Station, Memphis, Quantico, NAS Pensacola, Camp Pendleton (twice), Ft Gordon, Marine Corps Base, Okinawa (twice accompanied), and MCAGCC Twenty-Nine Palms during my twenty-six years of active duty. We traveled the world in the Far East together as she worked for the University of Hawaii and Pepperdine University (overseas), plus in her spare time, she was a jewelry-buyer for the Okinawa Marine Wives' Gift Shop. Many times, she alone maintained our family during my active-duty deployments including to the war in Vietnam, and other temporary duty, away. Somehow, she maintained this household including caring for and protecting a severely physically and mentally challenged young daughter (Karen) and accomplished these tasks frequently as we progressed through the Marine Corps ranks and assignments system until retiring from active duty in our beloved Corps of Marines.

Afterward, as our children searched and found a life away from our home, she was beside me through Upstate New York (Sheriff's Office), South Florida (Sheriff's Office), Guam (researching and writing a book), and in returning to our chosen South Carolina, returning to where we began our married life. She enjoyed travel, and we fondly reminisced on them all, frequently; she loved people and enjoyed being with others at home and abroad. She was an avid reader, and intently studied The Chicago

Manual of Style, which is why she could accurately and professionally assist me in writing books and articles through the last few years. Indeed, without her, there would not have been books and articles published under my name.

Sadly, COVID assisted in her demise, not that she contracted it, but because she could not receive adequate medical assistance during the pandemic. Her small-cell cancer could have been, and should have been, detected earlier had her chosen doctors not been otherwise distracted. It took a change in her voice and a visit to an ENT doctor to accidently discover her cancer mass. After a year and a half of chemo resulting in periodic hope only to melt away to despair, she fought the disease that would overcome her. In the end, she chose hospice care to assist her in traveling this new road of life, leading toward death. She maintained her spirit to the end. She was my last rose of summer, blooming alone, as the pedals fell one by one.

A great part of me, the part that allowed me to write, and accomplish those things I get credit for, just sailed away to a better place where she may touch the face of God, and inspire heavens angles as she has me and others during her time on this earth. Fair winds and following seas, my Lyn.

Ralph Stoney Bates
Major USMC (Ret)
Husband/Widower

The famous Marine Commandant, John Archer Lejeune is given credit for the phrase "Once a Marine, always a Marine." And my Marine Corps has adopted that expression as fact. So too then, as a young male Marine Corporal (like me) meets a young girl (like Lyn), they fall in love, and as a sergeant, he marries her; then, she is referred to as a Marine Wife. I submit, should that union exist throughout that Marine's career or time in service, as mine and many others did, then—"Once a Marine Wife, always a Marine Wife." My wife, now deceased was a Marine wife, and always will be a Marine wife. My claim is that she was unique. That will be for you, the reader, to decide. I simply will start this missive with this quote from *The Rifleman's Creed*, every Marine knows what that is: The Rifleman's Creed (also known as My Rifle and The Creed of the United States Marine) is a part of basic United States Marine Corps doctrine. Major General William H. Rupertus, USMC wrote it during World War II following the attack on Pearl Harbor between late 1941 and early 1942 explaining the uniqueness between a Marine and their rifle. The first line of that creed goes like this: *This is my rifle. There are many like it, but this one is mine.* That said, please meet my *Marine Wife, Lyn*: There are many like her, but this one is mine.

. . .

As I am now all alone attempting to close out these numerous tangible possessions of my deceased bride. I gather around the snapshots, portraits, documents, the real property, such as her clothing, jewelry, and other items associated with her, or the two of us, and as I sort through item after item, extemporaneously, am reminded of times, places, events, and people from our past. Each item evokes memories. The Shi-Shi dog statues from Japan, the water-jugs (miso-kami's) from Okinawa, the driftwood piece from Parris Island's Elliot's Beach, the enormous sea-shell and coral collection from the waters of Okinawa, and Guam, the photographs, especially the photographs and a myriad of other items that we, as a couple have collected over the last sixty-four years, stir instant, unrepressed memories.

As I hold, gaze upon, and reflect on some of the cherished items a surge of remembrances overwhelms my mind, body and soul of times and places shared with two lives well-lived. Some of these items chronicles times and events shared only by the two of us, others are memories of group settings, and I must decide what to retain, keep aside for our daughter, what to sell, and what to give away, and quickly start an undecided pile of items. Items collecting in this pile, I am just not ready to part from. Not yet!

While so engaged, slowly comes the obvious realization—memories are the only thing of lasting value. It's the intangible memories that will, in the final analysis, outlast the tangible belongings. It's the one thing of unique value which cannot be sold, bartered, or given away. As long as there's someone with a memory of my *Marine Wife, Lyn,* she will continue to live, if only in memories, her presence will be known and she will, indeed continue to live in someone's memories. As I write these words, I'm holding a photo someone snapped of me in Vietnam, and, of all things unimaginable, it is attached to my original R&R Hawaii ID card. Finding them in a small stack of photographs and other items she considered valuable, hidden away in a special place known only to her, I had no idea they still existed. Suddenly, those old memories kick in.

R&R card and photo of me in Vietnam

BACKGROUND

Vietnam is a place, a war, and an emotion, especially for those who fought that war, and for those who waited for their return. It was a country in Southeast Asia autonomous from other Southeast Asian countries, occupied by the French as colonist in the 1800s who renamed it as part of French Indo-China.

The country was occupied by the Japanese during World War II; whereupon, at wars conclusion, the French reemerged as colonist again, against the wishes of the people of Vietnam. Ultimately the French were defeated by a "people's army" and the country of Vietnam was divided into North and South Vietnam. Another war emerged between the North of Vietnam and the South of Vietnam which evolved into a war between a semi-democratic South and the Communist North, The United States and several allied countries intervened assisting the South against the North.

I was part of that war. Lyn maintained a home and family while I deployed to serve in combat, and to perform other duties during that war in Vietnam. It was the only war wherein the American participants, including those who had never served in Vietnam, but had served elsewhere were mistreated, chastised, maligned and harassed by a large number of American citizens when returning home from their foreign service. It had never happened before or since, and it is the reason Vietnam War Veterans still greet each other with the words, "Welcome Home!"

. . .

It was right after the TET Offensive of 1968, began winding down. I had returned to my criminal investigative duties, after participating in the ground defense of the Da Nang Air Base. We had made several engagements with the enemy. Contact was just south of the base. MPs and 1ˢᵗ Marine Air Wing "volunteers" from Tango Security (the volunteer group who not only performed their "day job," but volunteered to take up defensive positions around the Marine Corps side of the airbase when they were "off duty") and were eager to "do their thing," but eagerness was tempered by being somewhat disorganized and actually seemingly unprepared, yet, after preparing defensive positions, conducting briefings, running through a bit of rehearsals, making contact with adjacent units and assigning zones and sectors of fire, plus preparing positions and considering alternate positions for defense in case forward positions were overrun or neutralized, these young air-wing Marines did encounter the Viet

Cong (VC) insurgents and/or North Vietnamese Army (NVA) units in combat and did control and defend the south end of the air base Tactical Area of Responsibility (TAOR).

As proven many times in Marine Corps history, indeed the—*Every Marine is a Rifleman*, concept is real. It works. Commanding a hastily assembled composite "reserve rifle platoon" of Air Wing Marines, as opposed to combat infantry Marines (which gradually grew to about a hundred or so Marines of the Air Wing), was challenging and yet rewarding at the same time. Plus, it was down-right scary.

I was one of those volunteers, and was ultimately relived by a much more combat experienced lieutenant in order to return to my primary criminal investigator duties. Returning to the confines of the Marine Air Wing compound, my first task was obtaining a shower and getting into some clean clothes, plus needing to catch up on reading letters from my wife, Lyn. There was a stack of mail on my field desk. In the very first one I opened, which was about ten days old, she mentioned that she would like to meet in Hawaii for my R&R (rest and relaxation) and that she had found someone to keep our small children for the ten days it would take. In the last few weeks, I had forgotten that we had discussed the possibility of meeting in Hawaii halfway through my in-country tour it in our earlier letters.

Now several problems bugged me regarding R&R. First, all of my pay, except about thirty dollars a month, went to her. To Lyn. She had a house to maintain, and kids in school, medical expenses for one of our special-needs daughters, plus paying all the bills. If memory serves me correctly, I was still paying Al Bolognese Uniform Shop, in Quantico, for my officer uniforms.

I had completed a screening course at Quantico, Virginia and was promoted from sergeant to warrant officer (W-1) back in early 1964. Then recently, promoted to lieutenant. Lieutenants, even those like me with prior enlisted service didn't make a lot of money in 1967-68. Bluntly stated, I didn't think we could afford her round-trip airfare from San Diego to Honolulu. Then, even if we could squeeze that together, there was the hotel cost. Plus, the money for meals and sightseeing. If we could somehow stretch payments out—maybe, just maybe it could be accomplished; however, there was no lay-away plan for R&R. Things looked dim for a much-desired R&R. Second, when to do it. I needed my headquarters squadron unit to cut (write) military orders for Lyn so she could get the military discount from the airlines, and I had to plan it so that the duties and responsibilities of our criminal investigation department would continue to function properly. I expected a master sergeant inbound in early May. I felt that we needed to wait until then. But the money problem kept haunting me.

Sometime later, sitting in my hooch (building) still at my field-desk, glancing through an old *Time* or *Newsweek* magazine, my eyes fell on an ad for an American Express credit card. Frankly, I knew about the new VISA credit card, but I didn't have one, and I never had heard of the American Express card. Call me uninformed, or naïve; however, it simply wasn't on my radar. The requirements for the card had a minimum yearly income requirement which I didn't even come close to meeting, but I was foolish and bold, in that order. So, I drafted a hand-written letter, to the address listed in the magazine, explaining my situation and boldly asking for a salary exception, due to my current status, and I requested a credit card. My very first credit card.

Emboldened from that process, deeper in the same magazine, my eyes fell on an advertisement for the Outrigger Hotel on Waikiki Beach in Honolulu. Since I was grasping for straws, I might as well grasp for another handful. Yep! You guessed it. Drafting another hand-written letter asking for the possibility of a room for two with a beach view at a pauper's rate. Of course, I embellished on my status as lonely American service man in a far distant land, with a war ongoing and a wife that I missed very much (no embellishing there), so I fired off both letters knowing I'd never get a response. I was wrong.

I received an envelope from American Express and another from the Outrigger Hotel. Each came in the same batch of weekly mail on the same day about two weeks later. One contained a green American Express card with *Lieutenant Ralph S. Bates* printed across the face; the other was a welcome letter from Outrigger Hotel telling me I would have a room with an ocean view at the "R&R" rate. Translated: Cheap!

• • •

In May, 1968, Lyn departed San Diego for her first ever, airline flight. Around the same time-frame I departed Danang, Republic of Vietnam on a Pan Am flight with about 175 other eager soldiers, sailors, airmen and Marines for Hawaii, via Guam. I sat next to a soldier who was a last-minute replacement for his friend who had been killed in action just yesterday. He had the heartbreaking task of informing the man's wife, who was waiting for her husband in Hawaii. He was then to escort her home to California, to meet her deceased husband, for burial. He was best friends with both the dead soldier and his wife, now widowed. Stories like that were common. A wife arrives in Hawaii, goes out to meet him at the airport and he's not on the flight. To her shock, she learns he was killed. It was a common circulated story. Unfortunately, some of them true.

Arriving at the Honolulu airport about sundown and processing out for my days of R&R, I grabbed a cab bound for the Outrigger Waikiki Hotel. Lyn and I had agreed that I would meet her at the Outrigger. She had arrived earlier in the day and had managed to get to the hotel with no problems. The Concierge advised her to take a walk through the International Marketplace across the street from the hotel. This young Marine wife from Anniston, Alabama was very impressed with Waikiki.

I got to the room sometime between 2000 (8 p.m.) and 2100 (9 p.m.), it was almost dark. As I embraced my beautiful wife, before I even thought to sit my Valpak (issued suitcase) down, I was overwhelmed with emotion. The patio doors were open to the outside lanai overlooking the ocean, Hawaiian music was drifting up from the Royal Hawaiian Hotel next door and the red glow of an erupting volcano (okay, maybe it wasn't a volcano) was visible in the far distant horizon over a moon filled sea. Perfect! There really is a heaven on earth.

Armed with my new R&R Hawaii card, which identified Vietnam War returnees for R&R, my bride, Lyn and I had a fantastic, wonderful, memorable time in Oahu. I escaped the war zone for heaven on earth even if it was only for just a few amazing, wonderful days. All made possible because of a couple of stupid, brash, pleading (ok—groveling) letters asking for something for nothing and a couple of people receiving them who had a heart and empathy for a small Marine in a big, long-ago, war. It took us about six months to pay off the American Express bill. But we did pay it off with a smile on our faces.

While we were together in Hawaii, we mutually agreed to not even mention Vietnam or the war for the full seven or eight days. We saw the Don Ho show, went through the International Market Place many times, drove over the island to the Polynesian Cultural Center, attended a luau at the Royal Hawaiian Hotel, and roamed the new Ala Mauna Shopping Center. We visited the USS *Arizona*, more than one bar, had great food and a few Mai-Tai's and much of it was at greatly reduced prices due to the little R&R card displayed every time I talked to anyone (except Lyn) or ordered anything, anywhere. We had much enjoyable beach-time right behind our hotel and we rented a topless Jeep to tour all around the Island. We had a fantastic, wonderful vacation. We just lived. Just the two of us. My Marine Wife and me.

The last day finally came. Parting was sad. I had several more months to do on my tour of duty in Vietnam. Not easy parting. Damn hard. Lyn had to remain overnight to catch her flight back to San Diego the next morning, long after my Pan Am flight had departed. She chose not to see me leave. She fought back tears as our parting words to each other were, "See you later." I think I got back to Vietnam before she departed Hawaii. At least we had time together. We didn't ever talk about the next few months ahead of us. But I'm sure we thought about it, yet never revealed our thoughts of more separation-only revealing our love for each other and for our time together in our Hawaiian paradise. To this day, it remains the most memorable of lifes events.

Hawaii 1968

. . .

When Lyn made the decision to stop her chemo infusions, we knew what the outcome would be. Like Hawaii a little over fifty-years ago, we decided to not talk about it. We decided to simply live our last few months or weeks together as we had lived our lives together, and as we lived our R&R in Hawaii together. This time there was no beach, no Hawaii, no drive around an island, this was not R&R. We were alone together most of the time. Early-on, in this fight against cancer, we would go out with friends for lunch or dinner, attend meetings with various groups; however, as time passed and she grew weaker, we ceased excursions out except for medical necessities. As Lyn grew weaker, and weaker, caregiver services were required. Someone had to be with her if I were not present.

For a while, I'd continue to volunteer at Patriots Point Naval and Maritime Museum when we had a caregiver. I was with her when we did not. Some of the caregiver service providers were very good, while some were clearly attempting to work beyond their abilities. For her last eight weeks I was with Lyn 24/7 unless a quick run to the store or pharmacy was necessary. Someone was with Lyn all day, every day, and I was that person most of the time. Every night, I was with her, sleeping nearby.

As days passed toward a certain future, my admiration for this lady I married grew by leaps and bounds to exceptional levels. The resolute dignity, bravery, resolve, and attitude she exuded was remarkable and revealed her true self, deserving the highest level of respect and admiration any person can garner in this race we call human. It's remarkable the things remembered, the little things. I'd ask, "Would you like some water?"

She'd respond, "Yes, please." *Please!* So unnecessarily polite. So—Lyn. She lived her last days with exceptional dignity.

. . .

Some months earlier, we had sat together at the Medical University of South Carolina (MUSC) Cancer Center in Charleston, apprehensive, nervous, waiting for the doctor to say something other than introducing himself and his assembled colleagues. One could easily see that he was searching for words to start the conversation. When he did, he was blunt and to the point. The words alone sent tremors up and down my spine, my mouth tried to form words, but nothing emerged. "Mrs. Bates," he paused and composed himself, "Lyn, the biopsy reveals you have small-cell cancer that appears to be attached to the outside, rear of your lung." He again paused briefly, "I'm sorry," he added, "It's rather large," almost as an afterthought.

Our world seemed to be suspended in shock and disbelief. We had read, small-cell cancer cannot be "cured." The COVID-19 pandemic was enveloping the entire world, and now, this. This enveloped only us. I looked at my Lyn. She seemed to accept what the doctor had said. Quickly, the doctor began to suggest various options for us to consider, the most logical was chemo-therapy. It offered our best hope. Doing nothing was out of the question, and against Lyn's nature. Another battle loomed before my bride. Another obstacle of so many in her life to overcome. We departed the doctor's office in Charleston with weak optimism that grew stronger with each offered option and each series of medical appointments. As she had many times in her life, she'd fight.

. . .

A year or so before we were looking forward to our 60th wedding anniversary. We had plans, but something came up, something medical related. I required vascular surgery, while she had some medical malady that caused us to not make a plan for the actual 60th anniversary. So, we regrouped and planned to make it on our 61st and call it our 60th, by scheduling and paying for our first ever river cruise. It was to be a Danube River cruise with all the trimmings and we were anxious to get underway. Unfortunately, COVID cancelled that trip and, at the same time, it camouflaged routine medical appointments, canceling some, offering only virtual appointments for others. Not remembering the exact time and circumstances, my bride began to experience some mild breathing problems, real, not imagined and was unable to receive routine regular on-site appointments, especially pulmonary care exams. Instead, she relied mostly on community medical centers such as the one at State Road 41 and US-17 near our home in Mt. Pleasant, South Carolina.

It was during one of these appointments that a doctor suggested she see an Ear, Nose, and Throat (ENT) facility about her voice changing. It was becoming more high-pitched, rather than her usual normal voice. That visit to an ENT doctor caused the doctor to view, on a routine X-Ray of her voice-box area, an unusual mass in or near Lyn's lung. A later CT scan at MUSC confirmed a rather large mass and this particular biopsy confirmed small-cell lung cancer. Thus began an almost two-year odyssey of chemo-therapy, hope and despair, first at Roper, in Building 900 on Bowman Road, as it became known to us, while, much later at (MUSC) both downtown Charleston and at Mid-Town in Mt. Pleasant.

The treatment began and optimism grew. She would often prefer to drive herself to therapy, sometimes I would accompany her. While receiving chemical infusions three times a week, she continued to drive, shop, go out for lunches and dinners with friends, and—lose her hair. Once the hair loss became obvious, she made an appointment at The Healing Boutique at Roper St Frances Hospital in West Ashley and stated to the owner-operator: "Cut it all off!" She was beautiful with a bald head. She called it her "new hairstyle." She faced certain death attempting to live. Seemingly making light of the situation, while at the same time, we were more and more verbally reliving our times past, especially our Marine Corps days. Conversations about anything in the future were seldom broached and when it did arise, was quick and to the point. We often discussed our good life together, even some of the troughs in the ebb and flow of life we found ourselves in, she would brighten the days. Our good life was real! So badly did she fight to live. Once, we thought we had made it.

After few months of rather intensive chemo therapy several times a week, she was told by her oncologist at Building 900 that her cancer was "in remission." Our optimism skyrocketed! Per previous protocol, she then made an appointment with the MUSC radiation doctor. I accompanied her for that appointment. I'll never forget that day. The doctor sat us in her office with a big-screen computer in front of us, showing three different CT scans and, as she explained the confusing patterns on each scan, made the statement: "Lyn, you don't need radiation. There is nothing to radiate." We were in the preverbal "Seventh Heaven." Words cannot explain the intensity of the relief. We both were grinning like a jackass eating briars! We were beating the odds. Mere words escape me in my ability to relate the exhilarating feeling she must have had, for I certainly did. We walked out of that doctor's office on a cushion of air, feeling ten feet tall, yet light as a feather.

This news did not mean the cancer was gone. Small-cell cancer, we were told, cannot be cured, but sometimes it may be controlled giving the patient a small lease on more life. Anything, a week more, a month more, maybe. We were beginning to actually talk—future.

To celebrate, we decided to travel to Florida and visit our twice a year weekly time-share and, at the same time, also to visit with our daughter living nearby. We had a GREAT visit. Much of our conversations related to the future, not the past. The next time-share was to be in August, only a few months later. We even discussed another trip to our favorite vacation spot—Portugal. Obviously, we were on a "high!" We were like the proverbial "two kids in a penny-candy shop, with a dollar in our pockets," laughing, joking, making plans for something next year, until our bubble burst. As we were traveling from the visit with our daughter back to our time-share, Lyn's iPhone rang, she answered it. It was bad news. Totally unexpected! Immediately, we went into deep despair.

It was her radiologist doctor explaining to her that something happened. To this day, we don't know what, but the mass had grown to its original size. How this happened that we went from "There's nothing to radiate," to "It's back," in just a few short weeks, we were dumfounded. Her radiation doctor went on to explain that there was this new doctor at MUSC who was very good at treating cancer which had been previously treated without success. So, Lyn changed to MUSC for treatment.

At first, we were optimistic. During the very first infusion of chemicals, we were told it reduced the cancer mass by fifty-percent. It produced another "high!" Then, things began to change. Lyn became weaker and weaker the longer she was on the "new" treatment. My, appearing visibly healthy bride, went from totally ambulatory; able to drive, walk, etc., to needing first a cane, then, a walker, and finally, a wheelchair just to move around the house. Simply getting to and from the bathroom, the bedroom, or her favorite spot on the couch in our back sunroom became a major challenge even with my assistance.

A few times, usually in the nighttime, I'd need to call 911 for assistance. Once Lyn was having difficulty breathing, once she fell and I couldn't get her up. At least three times she went from our home to emergency rooms and from the emergency rooms to being admitted to the MUSC Hospital in

Charleston. The treatment was always good, but it was as she was being discharged from the next to the last time she was admitted, a bizarre event occurred. The discharging doctor, a female doctor at the hospital, standing in her room preparing her discharge papers as Lyn was getting dressed to depart, told us straight forward, "You are misusing the hospital." I couldn't believe it was said, and frankly, was too stunned to engage the doctor in conversation. I began to mentally analyze what happened. "Misusing? How does a sick person misuse a hospital?"

The day before, I believe it was, while Lyn was in her hospital room, in bed, the entire team of oncologist with that particular Charleston MUSC hospital visited Lyn in her hospital room. I was present. I wasn't sure of the purpose of the group meeting; however, the spokesperson began his verbal delivery by praising Lyn's MUSC Oncologist as to having the best plan for her treatment and that there was little the hospital could do to add to the treatment, or words to that effect. I often wondered if that group session and the discharging doctors' statement were connected. Now, I believe they were.

What I do know is that her treating oncologist began to reduce the amount of chemo drug in an apparent attempt to keep Lyn out of having to go to the hospital. Matter of fact, her chemo doctor at MUSC Midtown told us the reason for reducing the drug amount was to "keep Lyn out of the hospital." Several times the doctor would mention Lyn's age as "being in her 80s." She emphasized that Lyn was her "oldest" patient. And, several times the doctor mentioned that she didn't want to have Lyn going to the hospital. The reduced chemo amount ultimately led to the spread of the cancer. That is my belief. I believe it because, when CT scans revealed slight spreading of the cancer her oncologist began to increase the amount of the drug going into Lyn's body, but it is my belief it was too little, too late. I sincerely believe the effort to "keep her out of the hospital" was the reason for reducing the amount of the chemo. Reducing the amount of chemo allowed the cancer to spread. Then too, after the hospital stay, Lyn had asked if she could perhaps "take a brief break" from chemo infusions in an attempt to try to regain her stamina and strength, as Lyn had become very weak, needing a wheelchair to move about. My Lyn simply wanted to try to be more helpful in caring for herself. She hated being unable to even provide basic self-care for routine matters. It was her nature. We were told that such a brief break in chemo infusions was perhaps a proper thing to do. As I look back, I'm not sure.

I have asked the MUSC Hospital numerous times, in writing, did MUSC have a policy of discouraging cancer patients from being admitted to the hospital for maladies caused by their treatment for cancer. Never has a response been received. Now, it's too late for an answer.

. . .

My Marine Corps bride of sixty-three-years has faced numerous obstacles, trials and tribulations, in time overcoming each. She was born in February,1942, and about the time she began to attend school, she began to be physically/sexually abused. She grew up in an abusing home. She was abused by her father. Her own blood-related father physically abused his young daughter, his defenseless young child. His own child. Instead of being the loving, caring, protective father a man is supposed to be, he abused her.

Lyn told me the story over time. It made me want to confront the man; however, Lyn cautioned against such a move. Her attitude was, that he was a sick person. It started early when she was about six. She survived, fighting back in the only way she knew how by attempting to never be alone with her father. She attended a Woodstock grade school, which I believe was on Tenth Street near Woodstock Avenue in Anniston, Alabama. She could have simply ridden the school bus home going up Tenth Street; however, she'd walk all the way up Tenth Street, taking her time, avoiding any prospect of being alone with her father. She knew her mother would be preparing supper at a certain time, and it was that time she planned to arrive home.

When her family moved from East Anniston to a location referred to as Saks, she followed the same pattern of walking home—slowly. As she grew into her late pre-teens, and early teens, when he would attempt to abuse her, she began to actively physically resist and threatened to "tell on" him. She never stopped fighting back and, in the end, during her mid-teen-aged years, overcame that adversity by grabbing objects for protection and stating boldly, loudly and clearly, she would inform their minister and she would inform the police regardless of what might happen. After that highly emotional verbal and physical response; he left her alone. Lyn said she would not have informed the police because they would arrest him and her mother had no means of maintaining a home since she would have no income. But, she said, "He believed me." She always believed he had possibly transferred to one of her younger sisters.

That childhood trauma which no one should ever face, though it affected her from time-to-time, until she would briefly talk to me about it, and then again, put it behind her, always. Although this missive isn't about me, it's about my bride, but for clarity in relating information about her, occasionally I must inject a bit of my own upbringing and personal situational living events to clearly relate things in our mutual lives in more understandable fashion. After all, we were very close, as close as two people can be, and some of the rationale for our lifestyle was not only her uniqueness compared to me, but also our similarity in thoughts, words, and deeds with each other. As a child, Lyn was abused, and in a way, so was I, but I have never thought of it as physical abuse. Abandonment was more descriptive for relating my young life.

Lyn, as a preschooler and as a Junior High School student

. . .

When the Japanese bombed Pearl Harbor, I was three-and-a-half-years old living with my mother, her two sisters, her three brothers, and her father and mother (my Traywick grandparents). My living conditions were, a bit different from most, but certainly not all of normal society in those particular times, and in that particular place. While living with the Traywick's of Anniston, Alabama, and immediately before entering the Marines, most of my early life was lived with my grandmother Traywick in Alabama.

My father was in the Civilian Conservation Corps (CCCs) in the late 1930s and in the US Army from 1940-1946. My mother and father divorced in 1942. They remarried in 1946. To this day, I have never discovered why. During World War II, we (me and the Traywick's who were not in the military) lived in the home of my grandparents in rural Alabama along a very poverty-stricken countrified area called the Buttermilk Road. I even remember the address. It was Route 4, Box 38.

We lived in a weather-beaten house with cracks in the walls, a tin roof and no indoor plumbing. Instead, we had a deep-well for water and an outhouse to dispose of human waste. No electricity. We had oil lamps and a coal/wood burning fireplace. The kitchen had an iron wood-burning stove and an icebox. My grandmother washed clothing (and sometimes prepared food by killing and preparing a hog) in a large iron kettle full of boiling water in the back yard and clothes were sometimes washed in that same kettle, then were rinsed in a # 3 wash-tub and hung to dry on an outside clothes-line. I took my occasional baths in that # 3 wash-tub. Obviously, water was hand-carried from the deep well in the front yard.

I remember once when my grandmother tried to bathe me in that iron kettle. I screamed that she was attempting to boil me and have me for a meal. I'd seen the Tarzan movies. She gave up and always used the # 3 tub for my sometimes baths.

We had a four-to-six-acre field where we farmed some of it which we called a Victory Garden, and we used an old tin-roofed rickety barn where we raised chickens, pigs, and stalled a milk-cow alongside a big, mean, stubborn goat. We bought groceries, utilizing a ration book and a few dollar bills, at a country-store some mile or so from our house and we bartered (swapped) food with all our neighbors, Black, White, and Native (had a Cherokee family nearby known by my grandfather who was born in Cherokee, North Carolina), and my grandmother Traywick was, according to her stories, Choctaw or Chata, as the Choctaw pronounced their tribal name; however, she was raised by a Caucasian family with the last name of Byars living between Gordo and Reform, Alabama near the Mississippi state line. They told my grandmother she was Chata when she questioned her darker skin which caused her some grief in school.

So, I grew up early, very dirt-poor. During World War II, my father was, as I said, in the Army, while, on my mother's side, grandmother Trawick was my primary caregiver. My Trawick uncles were in the Navy and my only Bates uncle was in the Marines, all, including my father were overseas during the war. All serving in the Pacific. My mother left home to work in an aircraft factory somewhere in the Carolinas. Actually, I still possess a small cap she brought to me marked "Chimney Rock" in North Carolina.

My mother died when I was nine, almost ten-years-old, and my father, apparently couldn't take it, and he often simply abandoned me, to occasionally resurface at another location briefly, again and again, from my abandoned location, he'd send for me, and I'd go to his location. Finally, I tired of it and abandoned him. He left me alone for over a week after my mother died, and again in New Orleans after he asked me to join him. He left me alone for much more than a week without notice as I was attending McDonough # 16 grade school on St Claude Avenue in New Orleans. He had departed for LaGrange, Georgia to be with his mother. Alone, I earned enough money cleaning a nearby bar and shucking oysters to get a train ticket and went back to my grandmother in Alabama.

After a summer with my grandmother, I moved to LaGrange, Georgia at his request, attended Hillside Junior High School, failed and attended summer school, until I heard from my uncle, the Marine one, that he (my father) planned to abandon me again, leaving me with his mother, my other grandmother. We (she and I) simply did not get along, so, I beat him to the punch. I abandoned him by departing LaGrange and going back to my grandmother Traywick. He never sought, or sent for me after that. I was thirteen-years-old then. Often alone, traveling, moving, and adjusting from one place to another, most of my developing years. So, I guess God put Lyn and me together because we fit. Perfectly!

. . .

Lyn and I met on a 1958 Labor Day weekend in Anniston. We were both born in that town; however, because of my father and my vagabond lifestyle, I grew up in numerous locations, from Oklahoma, Georgia, Louisiana, Mississippi, and Alabama living with whoever would take me in. Of course, as previously mentioned, it was with my grandmother Traywick most of the time—until she signed for me to enter the Marines as I turned seventeen.

Being home on military-leave, a Marine friend Kenny Reeves suggested we don our uniforms and watch the parade. As the parade was passing, across the street (Noble Street) were two young girls, one in particular had the nicest smile. I smiled back and she gave a small wave just as the parade had passed and the crowd began to scatter and dissolve. We lost sight of the two girls.

I had a couple more days before having to report to my next duty station; however, during that time Lyn was very busy, deeply involved in multitasking research, attempting to find out who was this Marine (she had to ask what kind of uniform I was wearing) she waved at. It took her almost the entire two days and half a night to finally discover who I was, and I was leaving the next day. She contacted me on the telephone and asked me to stop by the Anniston High School football field the next morning before my bus was to depart later that day. She was a band member and they were practicing the next day. Stopping by that practice session, I met my future wife.

Being a barely twenty-year-old Marine Corporal who had dropped out of high school to enlist in the Marines, partially to escape poverty, I had just returned from an eighteen-month deployment in the Far East, stationed mostly in Japan and the Philippines, and she was a sixteen-year-old high-school senior. She turned seventeen five months after we met. I loved her from very early in our times together. Before long, we were both in love. We fell in love quickly, honestly, and forever!

Whenever I could manage, I departed my duty station (Beaufort Marine Corps Air Station and/or Marine Corps Recruit Depot, Parris Island), traveling to Anniston by any means available to be with the person I fell in love with. It was usually just for a weekend. We would fill the time together, going to movies, eating out at cafés, traveling to Cheaha Mountain State Park near Anniston, or attending her high school social functions. Once, her mother allowed us to drive to Atlanta where we went to see the Cyclorama and ate dinner at a place called Leb's Pigalle in downtown (Underground) Atlanta.

Eventually, before her eighteenth birthday, with her mother's written permission we were married at St Michaels and All Angles Episcopal Church in Anniston, on the nineteenth of December in the year of our Lord, nineteen-fifty-nine. Lyn made her wedding dress, designed and purchased the wedding cake, and selected and made (sewed) the bridesmaids dresses. John Willaman, a local Marine Corporal was my best man. Marine Sergeants Kovacs and Smith, two of my fellow Drill Instructors (DIs) from Parris Island came to Anniston to be escorts, and along with my best man, and with another local Marine friend, Kenny Reeves, formed the arch of swords as we exited the church. Lyn had told her mother we were to be married, period. And, if her mother would sign for her approval (required if under eighteen), she would stay home and finish high school. After her high school graduation in June, 1960, we moved into quarters aboard Parris Island in South Carolina to begin our life together. To coin a phrase, "We never looked back."

Linda "Lyn" Gale Bates and Ralph Stoney Bates
Exiting St Michaels Church 19 December 1959

. . .

BACKGROUND

Parris Island is in fact, an island connected to the mainland by a man-made causeway. It has been a training base for Marine Recruits enlisting east of the Mississippi River since 1917 and a basic training base for women enlisted Marines, plus other schools are located on the Depot. Its official title is Marine Corps Recruit Depot. In addition to the schools and the Recruit Training Regiment, it is a virtual city into itself. Housing for personnel stationed there are numerous and varied. Clubs, sports facilities, a food commissary and retail exchange shopping areas are sufficient for the families and military personnel assigned to the Depot.

My new bride, Lyn had never actually been alone in any living condition, although she relegated herself to being alone as much as possible outside her home because of "conditions" at home. She did spend time with both sets of her grandparents from time to time, but to be truly alone never happened until she arrived at Parris Island, married to a drill instructor. We arrived from her parents' home in Anniston onto Parris Island on a Sunday, and on Monday, Tuesday and Wednesday, of the following week, I was with the recruits at Elliot's Beach for preliminary field training. All drill instructors (D.I.s) from the four-platoon series, consisting of four platoons of 70-75 men each, were present as the entire series marched from their barracks, to Elliot's Beach, bivouacked overnight, and conducted field training before returning to their barracks, while for three days and nights Lyn was alone in our quarters, *adjusting* to military life.

More, *adjustments* followed. There were three DIs with each platoon. One DI had to be present with the recruit platoon 24 hours a day. Adding to the drama of life with a drill instructor, I had the "duty" every third day. That means every third day, I left Lyn at 0500 (5 a.m.) in the morning to report for daily work (duty), remained with the platoon when the other two DIs departed around 1700 (5 p.m.), remained overnight with the platoon and didn't return home until 1700 the following day. Lyn was alone every third day and night for an extended period of time. She accepted it as a Marine wife should, and most all wives of DIs did.

In September 1960, Hurricane Donna tested Lyn's stamina as a new Marine bride. Parris Island had gone through Hurricane Gracie in September 1959, which devastated the island and actually delayed all recruit training for almost two weeks. Donna was on the way, and Parris Island prepared. All military dependents living in military housing on the island were evacuated to the Depot Headquarters Battalion Barracks, a large brick reinforced billeting and office structure, where they remained for two days until the storm approached, hit, and passed. It was her first experience of several events. Being evacuated to an unfamiliar location, being alone with a hundred or so other women, most with accompanying children from babies-in-arms to school-age teens, and the taste of mess-hall (military dining facility) chow, which she thought was great cuisine. All evacuees ate three meals each day in the mess-hall. By the way, she was five-months pregnant at the time. I do remember either uttering or thinking some sort of words resembling, "I think I have a real Marine Corps wife," when she and I returned to our quarters L-9, after the all-clear announcement. I had been with barracks-confined recruits at the rifle-range barracks before, during, and immediately after the hurricane. Several hundred recruits, in one barracks filling four squad-bays, and two drill instructors, one topside and the other below throughout the passing hurricane. I was topside.

After attending and completing Drill Instructors School at Parris Island in April 1959, I was a Sergeant (E-4), Drill Instructor with Kilo Company, Second Recruit Training Battalion. Lyn and I arrived on Parris Island as a married couple in early June 1960. We were poor as a church-mouse, and as happy as a pig-in-slop. In early 1961, I was completing my tour as a DI, and was transferred to serve in the Military Police aboard Parris Island. Our first child was born at the US Naval Hospital, Beaufort, in 1961, a daughter, Deborah.

We lived in a very small duplex at Parris Island (quarters L-9, Ribault Village) destined for married corporals and sergeants. It had two small bedrooms, a living room and small kitchen, and one bathroom. It was heated by a gravity-fed oil heater in the living room. We had to purchase the oil. It had no air conditioning. The small bathroom was squeezed between the two bedrooms. We purchased meager basic furniture from Stucky Brothers and Hart at Laurel Bay. That's the same furniture store we have here in Mt. Pleasant. They sold mostly to Marines and Sailors. The kitchen was small and the refrigerator was a very small one sitting on a kitchen counter. It had two ice trays in the freezer compartment and getting anything else in the freezer was next to impossible. But Lyn's big concern was baby formula. No room for more than one bottle at a time along with grocery items that required refrigeration. This situation set the stage for our first family crisis. It went something like this…

. . .

"I just don't see how we can keep baby formula in this tiny little box they call a refrigerator," she mused matter of fact.

"I admit it's small, but it's what we get. Sergeants and all corporals' quarters, have this little refrigerator. To get a bigger one, we'd have to buy it out in town. We don't have the money," I responded to my young, wife, now a young mother.

"Then we can't buy meat at the commissary unless we do it every day," she emphasized. "I can't keep the little bit of meat that we can barely afford, other things needing refrigeration, and baby formula in this thing." Then she simply started to cry. "I'm sorry," she uttered softly. "We'll manage," she finished. I felt terrible. As a sergeant, we simply didn't rate a larger refrigerator. Hell, the kitchen wasn't really large enough for one. The quarters were small. Very small. So was a sergeant's pay, even a married one.

The Marine Corps staff at the headquarters in Washington, DC had decreed that there would be a recruiting decrease. Manpower levels were to be reduced in the Marine Corps. The Recruit Training Regiment at the Marine Corps Recruit Depot at Parris Island, South Carolina, would drop in numbers. The number of recruits and number of drill instructors would be decreased. Orders went out for interested drill instructors to submit requests for reassignment to fill other vacancies. One caveat was to have at least 18 months on the drill field as a drill instructor to apply for transfer. Those not applying would be involuntarily reassigned. There was a posted need for sergeants in the military police (M.P.) at Parris Island and the Marine Corps Air Station, Beaufort. I applied for the M.P. at Parris Island.

Training involved a quick two-week trip to Fort Gordon, Georgia, attending the School of the Provost Marshal General. Then, I and three other sergeants, also being transferred to the M.P., had some local training administered by a seasoned M.P. Gunnery Sergeant at Parris Island.

After training, I was assigned as a shift sergeant supervisor of military police. Since my wife and I had our first child, a girl born in February, the early March transfer to the military police was timely and beneficial for home life. D.I. duty called for working six days a week and having overnight duty every third night. Very tough on married life. The assignment to a 12-hour shift, on duty as an M.P. and 12 hours of standby in the barracks. Then, get 36 hours off. Having been at the new job for about three weeks, military police duty was enjoyable and familiar as, I'd been a military policeman in Japan years earlier while stationed at the Naval Air Station, Atsugi, Japan. But, for weeks, the size of that refrigerator continued to be a big problem. Almost every other day, one of us, usually Lyn, made a commissary run just to buy one pound of ground meat, chicken, or flank steak—the cheapest meat in the store.

Something had to be tried. Dressing for work, I said to my wife, "Sweetie, tell you what. I'll go up to the warehouse and just see if they have anything bigger than this," pointing to the little refrigerator that now contained a single ice tray in a little freezer box and had a very small amount of refrigerator storage; it was stuffed with baby bottles and a pound of ground meat.

"Maybe they'll have one we can get," I said.

"They can only say no," she responded, smiling. I could feel she wanted to say something else, so I hesitated departing. "You know, you don't really have to. Let's forget it. We'll get by somehow," she reflected. "Even if we could afford to buy one or get a bigger one from the housing warehouse, where would it go? They'd be required to cut out a section of the kitchen counter. They couldn't do that. Nobody would dare do that to government housing."

As this story continues, at this juncture of time and at this place with this event, I'd like to switch this narrative to extract and insert this story directly from one of my previous publications titled *Short Rations For Marines*, and use that medium, which was largely written by my bride, with my assistance, from our recollections from our time, in that place, so long ago at Parris Island. She had verbalized our recollections in much more clarity than me; therefore, explaining it best, as she clearly remembered that refrigerator and how it came into our possession. So, previously written material, from my bride's recollection, so we cut and paste. This is Lyn speaking then, Here goes.

. . .

. . . Dressing in his uniform, applying his M.P. armband on his left sleeve, he fastened the white pistol belt with a white pistol holster attached, around his waist, attached the lanyard with a brass whistle at the end around his right shoulder and placed the white helmet liner with its distinctive red and yellow stripes on each side and a golden eagle, globe and anchor (the Marine Corps emblem) on the front, on his head. Then he kissed his wife and departed for his 24-hour duty, via the warehouse. His wife's voice called out to him, "They can only say no!" And, it continued ringing in his ears.

He pulled up in front of the warehouse near the Triangle area and went inside. He saw a corporal at a desk and approached him with his request. The corporal told him to see the "Gunny" and pointed toward the office. He started toward it just as the Gunnery Sergeant stepped out the door. "This is not going to be good," he said to himself. The gunny was frowning; actually, he had a scowl on his face. His eyes had a mean look. He had a white T-shirt on with utility trousers and boots. No cover (hat) and no shirt. It was hot in the warehouse.

"What the hell you want?" he asked sarcastically. He was a big man, tough and aggressive looking.

"Gunny, I was wondering . . ." he hesitated. "I live in Ribault Village and we just had a baby. I stopped by to see if there was any chance of getting a larger refrigerator. You see . . ."

"Who the hell are you?" the gunny asked as he placed his massive hands on his hips, staring the sergeant square in the face, maybe six inches away.

"I'm just asking if I can get a larger refrig..." The gunny cut him off with a wave of the hand.

"I don't see any rocker under those three stripes, sergeant. You ain't no staff sergeant."

"Okay, Gunny."

"Don't 'okay Gunny' me, asshole!" The gunny pointed a finger in his face.

"It's Gunnery Sergeant! You got me?" He was yelling and red faced. The sergeant looked over at the corporal who looked away and pretended to make a telephone call. "You M.P.s thinks the sun rises and sets on your ass, don't you? You think people will just give you anything because you wear an armband and carry a gun. Don't you?"

"No, Gunnery Sergeant. I was just asking."

The sergeant turned to leave. "Don't turn your back on me when I'm talking," the gunny shouted.

"I'm sorry, Gunnery Sergeant." There was a brief silence.

"Get the hell out of my warehouse. I don't like M.P.s and I don't like assholes. You're both." Then in a somewhat quiet voice, the gunny said, "It'll be a cold day in hell before I give a damn M.P. Sergeant a staff NCO's refrigerator." The sergeant turned and departed.

Guess we don't get a bigger refrigerator, he thought as he drove to the M.P./Guard Company in the red brick building near the "Iron Mike" statue, went inside, drew his weapon and ammunition from the armory, got his ticket book, flashlight and M.P. (police) club from storage and reported to relieve the on-duty supervising sergeant. He was still smarting from the ass-chewing by the gunny at the warehouse as he was briefed by the outgoing sergeant.

He took over the duty at 6 p.m. and checked in on the radio at the main desk sergeant's station. He then went out in front of the building to inspect his three roving patrolmen and their vehicles and equipment. Finding everything in order, he drove to the main gate to check the gate detail. All was well. Heading back toward the M.P. station, he stopped and went into the C.I.D. (criminal investigation department) office, above the fire station, just to check in with them before he continued back to the desk sergeant's station. His supervision responsibility was over a sergeant and four men at the main gate, three roving patrols in three vehicles, a supernumerary and a radio dispatcher/operator.

The patrol force had one patrolling the recruit areas, male and female and the main boulevard from the gate to the docks, another patrolled at weapons battalion, the ranges, Elliott's Beach, the trailer park and Wake Village and a third around Page Field, the ammo bunkers, officer housing and the headquarters area, including the MCX (Marine Corps Exchange), bank, commissary and the commanding general's quarters. He had, in addition to the supernumerary in the desk sergeants' area, eight men who were in the barracks, with no duty assignment at this time. Sometimes men need to be relieved; sometimes, special details are required, such as the raising and lowering of the colors, parking or security details. Occasionally, extra men are needed for incidents that may arise. He was to be on-duty supervisor for 12 hours and in the barracks on standby for 12 hours. Then he'd get his 36 off.

It was a typical night. A report came in of a missing recruit, who had run away from his barracks sometime after supper. A fight had broken out at the enlisted club. The gate reported a drunk civilian attempting to enter the base in his vehicle. The Beaufort County Sheriff's deputies took that one. A domestic disturbance at the staff NCO quarters in Wake Village, a vehicle accident near weapons battalion and a "Peeping Tom" in the female Marine recruit area. Typical slow evening.

The officers club closed up, and he was required to do a security check after closing, accompanied by the club's officer. The enlisted club closed and patrol number one stood by while club management secured the club and did a money drop at the bank. He decided to drive out to Weapons Battalion and check on the vehicle accident. He noticed the staff NCO Club was still open but not many cars were parked there. The accident was not major, but one person was taken to the Beaufort Naval Hospital as a precaution. He drove back to the desk sergeant's place of duty and on-the-way noticed the staff NCO club appeared closed but two cars were still parked in front parking area. He would check that out after filing the injury report from the traffic accident.

It was near midnight when he got in his vehicle, started down the main drag of Boulevard d' France and noticed car headlights coming from the vicinity of the staff NCO Club, through the second recruit training battalion area. That vehicle appeared to be travelling at a high rate of speed, screeching its tires and burning-rubber as a hard left turn was made onto Boulevard d' France. It was heading toward the main gate and drifting from one side of the wide boulevard to the other. He hit his red flashing lights, radioed the main gate to stop incoming traffic and warned of an apparent drunk driver heading toward them. He pulled directly behind the weaving vehicle, but its driver would not stop. One other patrol unit notified him that it was responding from Page Field to assist. At Horse Island, halfway to the main gate, the driver suddenly pulled off the road into the dark, isolated picnic area. He pulled the M.P. vehicle in behind and slightly to the left of the stopped car, placed his headlights on high beam, radioed in the stop, got his flashlight and ticket book and got out of his vehicle. Being very cautious, he unsnapped his holster, placed the ticket book under his left armpit, holding the flashlight in his raised left hand and slowly started to approach the stopped car. It was pitch black. No other traffic anywhere was visible.

The occupant/driver of the stopped vehicle opened his door and my Marine sergeant husband yelled, "Stay in the car! Don't move. Show me your hands." The occupant placed one foot on the ground. "Now!" he yelled, as he drew his pistol and dropped his ticket book to the ground. With his left hand, the sergeant shined his flashlight into the face of the seated driver, who was halfway out of his car. "I have a loaded weapon on you. Step out of the car. Keep your hands where I can see them!" He took two or three steps toward the idling car with its half inside, half outside driver/occupant, and then stopped. He could hear the siren of the responding back-up patrolman some two miles away, back toward the parade ground. Since the driver was still seated in the car and he couldn't see his hands, he decided to wait for his back-up. "Stay there! Don't move!" he warned the driver again, pointing the pistol in his general direction and keeping the flashlight beam on the driver's occasionally revealed face—and finally his now visible hands.

About a week prior to that, he had stopped a weaving car in almost the same spot. It was very early in the morning, about 2 a.m. It had a blue officer's tag on the front and rear bumper and a single occupant, an officer, driving. Foolishly, he had walked right up to the driver's door, and the next thing he knew, he was looking directly into a small handgun being held by the driver. He threw his ticket book at the face of the driver, hit the deck (ground) and rolled behind the car, attempting to remove his pistol from its holster at the same time. His heart was going a mile a minute. He was very frightened and scrambling and crawling to get to the other side of the stopped car. Then, he heard the laughter.

The lieutenant had exited the car and was standing up, weaving around, trying to maintain balance and to use his little pistol-like cigarette lighter to light his dangling cigarette. The sergeant was furious. He apprehended and cuffed his first officer. The next day, he was standing at attention in the commanding general's office right next to that same lieutenant. The sergeant was asked to tell his side of the incident. He did and was dismissed. He never saw that lieutenant again.

So, he was especially cautious on this traffic stop. Now, he could hear the approaching patrol just about half a mile back. He looked at the face of the man in the glare of his flashlight. Looks somewhat familiar, he thought. The occupant remained sitting with his hands on top of the open door, but leaned out into the full glare of the flashlight and headlights of the patrol vehicle. He looked directly at the Military Police Sergeant and smiling a stupid-ass wide grin, he said in a rather loud, slurred, slow speech pattern, "Hey! Sarge! Buddy! What size refrigerator was that you wanted?" He paused briefly. "Buddy!"

This event really did not end with the warehouse Gunnery Sergeant's proclamation in that dark picnic area as the back-up patrol arrived. The Military Police Sergeant took the Gunnery Sergeant home to his wife and kids (common procedure in the 1960s) after securing his vehicle in the picnic area. He logged the incident into his log book and made a verbal report of the incident to the provost sergeant.

A few days after the incident, carpenters from base maintenance suddenly arrived at our quarters causing me to ask him, "Who sent these guys?"

His somewhat unbelievable response was, "Beats me!" They explained they were to make adjustments in the kitchen. Quite skillfully they cut out a section of the counter top and cabinet in the kitchen.

I asked, "Hon, could you explain to me why they are doing this?"

His response was, "I guess it's for a cold day in Hell, Sweetheart!"

That above was Lyn's narrative work describing the refrigerator incident in the Anthology, *Short Rations For Marines*. Although we made further edits before finally publishing, hers was a very accurate descriptive rendition of *The Refrigerator*. Admittedly, much more accurate than mine.

A couple of hours later, while Lyn was cleaning up some of the sawdust they had missed wiping up, the warehouse corporal arrived, in a covered truck, with two privates and brought in—to us, a rather large refrigerator (it was still small, but much larger than the one they hauled away, but not really a big one) and installed it in our kitchen. It fit perfectly. The corporal was grinning a big, wide, stupid-looking grin the whole time like the Curly character of the *Three Stooges*. It was, a nice refrigerator. Sometime, many weeks (or months) later, I told her in detail how we came to receive it. Lyn loved that refrigerator and has often verbally repeated that event.

. . .

Late in 1961, the crisis in Berlin caused me to be transferred back to the drill field, serving in Item Company, Second Battalion, training one more platoon. Suddenly, the Corps was in a build-up manpower mode. I don't know how Lyn did it, but, during our time at Parris Island in 1960 and 1961, she stretched our meager basic-pay to pay all our bills, feed us with commissary food, and maintain our beat-up Chevrolet, owned by a local credit agency. Lyn paid that bill each month also. Please understand, during most of these times. I was an (acting) sergeant, pay grade E-4. It wasn't until after I was transferred to the MPs that I received a promotion to sergeant, pay grade E-5. [In 1960, the Marine Corps changes its rank structure adding Lance Corporal as an E-3, and adding ranks E-8 and E-9. So, as a result everyone currently in whatever rank became an acting-whatever, until promoted to the next higher grade.] Once early on our Parris Island time, we didn't even have enough money to reregister our car causing our registration to expire, so it sat off-base in an impound lot for a couple of months until Lyn saved enough money to reregister it. Without a car, I wondered how we could make it bumming rides. Again, my bride showed she had "the right stuff."

She would walk to the Depot Commissary and Marine Corps Exchange (MCX), get what we needed and could afford and walk back home. She got up on all my work-days to prepare breakfast before I walked across a grassy field and reported for 0600 (6am) DI duty, and later for M.P. duty. She made friends with our neighbors, we fished and crabbed in a small place called Gibbs Island, out near Page Field, and she prepared picnic lunches for the picnic area at Horse Island. We'd have picnics with and without our neighbor/friends. She even asked the Company Chief Drill Instructor, Master Sergeant Hugo Black's wife, if we could have their old wringer-tub type clothes-washer as they were buying a new, more modern washer. We got it and Lyn no longer had to go to the community washeteria at Page Field to wash and dry our clothes. Times were hard, but she made them much better. She never complained. She loved the title, Marine Wife.

. . .

In November 1961, we were transferred to the Naval Air Station, Memphis, Tennessee, where we rented a small duplex off Navy Road in the community of Millington. I was an instructor with the Marine Aviation Detachment of the Naval Air Technical Training Center. We made good friends. Tom and Nellie Berry, he was a Staff-Sergeant, and they became our best friends at that time in our Marine Corps career. We attended a small Episcopal Church out in the country with a Rector by the name of Stoney. We found out it was his father William or "Bill" Stoney who baptized our Ralph Stoney, Senior. Me!

BACKGROUND

The Naval Air Station, Memphis is located near the city of Millington, Tennessee. It housed the Naval Air Technical Training Center which managed various schools for enlisted Sailors and Marines. Within the command structure was the Marine Aviation Detachment to which I was assigned. Nearby is the US Naval Hospital.

Our son Ralph Stoney Jr. was born, at the US Naval Hospital, Memphis in 1962. An interesting and life-long physical malady occurred after the birth of our son. Lyn developed an allergy to onion, and all the onion family except garlic. It was strange; however, it is fact. It took us many months to figure out what was making her sick so often. As time passed, it became a more and more of an acute allergy, oftentimes very debilitating. It persisted all her life and caused some unfortunate occurrences in our social life. Actually, some life altering occurrences.

I had earlier applied for a commission via the enlisted commissioning program and was "shot down," (rejected) the first time. The enlisted commissioning program, at that time, required an Associate's Degree, or an Associate's Degree Equivalent, which consisted of a series of college-level written exams conducted under supervision. Applicants must pass that testing before being allowed to attend officer Testing and Training (T&T) at Quantico's Officer Candidate School. That school had a 30% failure rate. I have no idea the failure rate of the Associates Degree Equivalent Test. I did not pass that series of tests.

However, in early 1963, my Captain, a Marine by the name of Tim O'Brien encouraged me to apply again, this time for the warrant officer program. Relating that information to Lyn, she never let up. Lyn insisted I apply. Each day, as I arrived home from work, I'd hear, "Have you applied yet," therefore, naturally, I did apply. Between my captain and my wife, I dared not to apply. The captain guided me into applying for the new, I believe it was the 6720 MOS, which was the military occupational specialty code for Airborne Intercept Officer, or Operator (AIO) program for the new F-4 Phantom jet fighter/interceptor entering the Marine Corps inventory. They had zero AIOs. He was a smart captain. I was accepted even though I didn't meet the qualifications of having an Associate's Degree. The Corps really needed those AIOs.

On the sad day that President Kennedy was killed in Dallas, I was notified by a phone call from Headquarters Marine Corps of my acceptance into the Warrant Officer Screening Course at Quantico, Virginia. For the first time my bride and I were to be really separated. I had told her, before we married, there would be separations. She expected it. When I was sent to the Provost Marshal General's School at Fort Gordon, Georgia from Parris Island, she accepted it. She rationalized it as part of being a Marine wife. But I came home to Parris Island from Fort Gordon on the single weekend I was attending the two-week school there. This particular separation, while attending the warrant officer screening course was to be much longer. Dependents were not allowed to accompany the Marine. People failed that course in sizeable numbers. Candidates were not allowed to have accompanying family members join them until they had passed the screening course and were eligible for promotion to the Warrant rank as a Warrant Officer (W-1).

BACKGROUND

Marine Corps Base/Marine Corps Schools, Quantico, Virginia was and is the premier training base for new officers and those wishing to become Officers of Marines I attended the 5th Warrant Officer Screening Course, The Basic School and the FBI National Academy aboard this sprawling Marine Base separated by

I-95 and US Highway 1. Quantico Town is distinctive as the only American city solely within a military base. The National Museum of the Marine Corps, where Lyn and I visited often and where we conducted many book-signings for some of our books is near the main gate of Quantico, in Triangle, Virginia.

Lyn and another Marine wife, whose husband was also selected to attend the Screening Course hooked-up and moved in together, so while two wives and four kids cohabitated, all us geographic-bachelors headed for twelve-weeks of "screening" at Quantico as a member of the 5th Warrant Officer Screening Course conducted by Major A.W. (Red Dog) Keller who made it a rather interesting engagement of our times. I think I still have some of the blisters, yet to heal. We started with near 220 candidates and graduated only 169 to be warrant officers, commonly called "lipstick-lieutenants" because of the red stripe across the brown (second lieutenant) bar. Graduate we did! Had the bars placed on my collar by none other than my bride, Lyn who had arrived a few days before and was staying at the base guest house aboard Quantico with our two young kids in tow, making it a point to attend our graduation ceremony.

We accomplished two feats almost simultaneously. We rented a place to live in the housing area called Melrose Garden's in Triangle, Virginia surrounded by dozens of second lieutenants and newly minted warrant officers. Suddenly, without any training or indoctrination, my bride is an officer's wife surrounded by dozens of similar wives. Actually, the warrant officer's wives did receive some informal instructions from a couple of officers and their wives who were instructors at The Basic School. An interesting development occurred during the wife's instruction classes.

When Lyn arrived at Quantico, she had reserved a couple of rooms at the Hostess House or Guest House (as I think it was then called), and having little to do before my graduation, being a prolific reader, she read anything she could find around the guest quarters; papers and magazines, anything laying around the accommodations was fair game for Lyn. Issues of *Marine Corps Gazette*, *Leatherneck*, the base newspaper, and other publications contained articles regarding the testing of a new and innovative weapons system. Lyn read with some interest articles regarding the Stoner Arms Weapons System that was currently being tested aboard Quantico.

Later, after our warrant officer graduation, the wives were receiving some instructions from a couple of captains and their wives. One of the captains instructing the wives made a comment about the system being tested, and Lyn corrected one of his stated assumptions, causing some awkward moments until Major "Red Dog" Keller appeared on the scene. Listening to the difference of opinion between the captain and Lyn, the major stated, "Better go back to the drawing board, captain, she's right." When it was discovered from other sources, she was correct and the captain was incorrect, she received a heartfelt apology. She suddenly had her admirers after that. She was cornered at several social functions with officers asking her questions about the weapons systems, while all of us "lipstick lieutenants," immediately after graduation and swearing in as warrant officers, headed out to the other side of I-95 to check-in for grooming and grinding, Marine Corps style.

After twelve weeks of The Basic School at Camp Barrett, which almost every Marine Corps officer must complete, we back-seat-driver candidates received orders to Naval Air Station, Pensacola, Florida for me to be trained to fly in a fighter jet, sitting in the back seat. Once at Pensacola, we rented a small duplex in Warrington, adjacent to the air station. Lyn, along with the other Marine warrant officers' wives received an invitation from the wife of the admiral to attend a tea at her quarters. Dressed in hat and gloves, Lyn enjoyed visiting the admiral's wife who had all the new warrant officers' wives in her quarters for tea, or whatever. We Marine warrant officers were an oddity for the Navy at Pensacola. Seems everyone was curious about us. Lyn was taking care of our two toddlers while, at the same time, she would also get together with the other wives occasionally for informal talk sessions. Just getting to know each other. We took our two kids to the beach often, ate out most of the time, and enjoyed our brief time in Pensacola, Florida, especially since we were drawing temporary additional duty (TAD) pay in addition to our regular pay.

BACKGROUND

Naval Air Station, Pensacola, Florida is the primary training base for Navy, Coast Guard, and Marine Corps pilots. It is also the home base for the famed Blue Angeles Flight Demonstration Squadron, plus other operational squadrons. With the closure of the Naval Air Technical Training Center (NATTC) at Millington, Tennessee (NAS Memphis), Pensacola has absorbed all Naval Air Technical Training for the sea services. Its location on the coast of the Florida panhandle, near Mobile, Alabama, gives it ideal weather most all year. The sole exception being occasional hurricanes.

In the meantime, my apprehensions about not being qualified, came to pass as we began the academic portion of Ground School, a prerequisite before getting near an airplane. Another new warrant officer, Bob "Yogi" Price and I simply didn't have the wherewithal, background, etc., to get through the academic portion of the ground-school. Both of us were high-school dropouts and both of us were in classrooms with VMI grads, Citadel grads, West Point and Annapolis grads, etc., and us. Me and Yogi. When at the end of each week—testing came, and we had not a clue of the difference between quadratic equations and a spelling bee. To respond to the fifty-question multiple choice test, Yogi chose the c column while I just danced around the four choices, blindly filling in any spot chosen. Yogi failed and got orders to Camp Pendleton, while I advanced to physics. At the next weeks test, I picked the c column.

Before arriving at Camp Pendleton a few weeks behind Yogi, Lyn and I took our two kids in tow and made our trip a cross-country vacation, travelling to our new adventure. We visited Meteor Crater, the Grand Canyon, Carlsbad Caverns, Old Albuquerque in New Mexico, and the Painted Desert. Arriving at Camp Pendleton, I was assigned to the base brig as security officer working for Major Lee Hardee.

. . .

BACKGROUND

Camp Joseph H. Pendleton, in San Diego County of Southern California was activated in 1942 from the purchase by the government of the sprawling Santa Margherita Ranch. The ranch house is still the living quarters of the commanding general of the base. At the time we arrived in the summer of 1964, the base housed the entire 1st Marine Division (Reinforced) and numerous base supporting units, spread throughout several smaller camps scattered across the large base, and around the area of concentration known as main-side. Adjacent to the base is the Fallbrook Naval Weapons Station, while, across I-95 was the Del Mar area where amphibian tractors (Am Tracs) of the division were located.

Numerous housing areas dotted the base for enlisted and officers; however, most personnel stationed there lived in Fallbrook, Vista, Escondido, Oceanside, and Carlsbad. Some personnel lived as far north as San Clemente, and as far south as San Diego. There was a Naval Hospital aboard Camp Pendleton as well as the large Balboa Naval Hospital in San Diego. At the time we were stationed there, Camp Elliott, a training base south of Camp Pendleton was preparing to close as the US Naval Retraining Command. It was a naval confinement facility where the term correctional custody was coined and practiced.

Although I applied for base housing, due to unavailability we moved into a nice rental house in Vista while awaiting base quarters. Lyn had discovered she was pregnant. In November 1964, a daughter was born. She was a Rubella Syndrome (German-Measles) child as they were called then. In the 1960s throughout the nation there was an outbreak of Rubella Syndrome births caused by the pending mother carrying the unborn child being exposed to this new strain of measles. *Congenital rubella syndrome (CRS) is an illness in infants that results from maternal infection with rubella virus during pregnancy. When rubella infection occurs during early pregnancy, serious consequences–such as miscarriages, stillbirths, and a constellation of severe birth defects in infants–can result* (Center for Disease Control). We quickly discovered she was deaf, and began to manifest symptoms of a severely physically and mentally handicapped baby. I was advised by one doctor to "get out of the Marine Corps," because we would not be able to care for our child while on active duty as a Marine.

To say we were devastated would be an understatement. We were also confused. Our child, Karen Denise Bates was very difficult to care for. We did get some assistance. Lyn would drive her to San Diego attending basic child-treatment and testing at Balboa Naval Hospital and to other outside doctors and therapist, as far north as UCLA Medical Center. We had expenses we had not anticipated, and once we actually had to ask the Navy Relief Society for assistance to get through one particular month financially. For the first time I was afraid we would not receive any assistance from any other source and quickly discovered we actually didn't have the income to place her in any of the known treatment facilities anyway. We weren't even sure where to search for assistance or advice. Essentially, we were alone with our dilemma, lost in an unknown and unnatural world.

Through all these times of despair and turmoil, Lyn took primary care of Karen while I performed my duties at the brig. Then came another separation. In September 1966, I was to attend The Institute of Correctional Administration at The American University in Washington, DC. They (the University) had said the class was to start on a particular date in September. Arriving at American University, I was told the class was to start on that particular date in October. Someone had made a mistake. I reported this fact to Headquarters Marine Corps at Henderson Hall, across the river on the Virginia side. Solution: Assignment to Congressional Correspondence Branch at Headquarters Marine Corps, Henderson Hall working for Colonel Dave Severance of Iwo Jima fame. Instead of four weeks away from Lyn, it turned into eight. While I resided in an apartment near the classroom on 14th Street, alone, my Lyn handled the situation at home. I finally completed the Correctional Administration Course and returned to Camp Pendleton.

Eventually, we moved aboard base into junior officer's quarters in an area known as De Luz Housing. Karen took almost all our time and effort. Lyn had formed several friendships on and off-base, and some of them would assist with Karen while Lyn and I, along with Deborah and Stoney, junior would take a much-needed mini-break. We'd go camping in the Julian Mountains, spend time on the beach at Del Mar, or visit several of the wineries nearby giving out free samples. Southern California wineries were much appreciated.

There was one other brief unplanned separation. I had been tasked with escorting Navy and Marine Corps prisoners from various brigs on the west coast to the US Naval Disciplinary Command (it was called "The Castle") at the Navy Base in Portsmouth, New Hampshire. Prisoners would be collected at the Marine Corps Air Station at El Toro, California where I and my detail of eight Marines as guard-escorts would board them onto a C-130 Marine transport aircraft and fly them to Pease Air Force Base near Kittery, Maine. We made one stop at Great Lakes Navy Base in Illinois to pick up more prisoners destined for Portsmouth. Marines from Portsmouth would meet the aircraft on the tarmac and take custody of them.

We (my detail and I) would then tag-along with the crew to a small seafood place in Kittery where we'd deliver six to eight cases of Coors Beer (you could only get Coors west of the Mississippi River), and pick up two crates of Maine lobsters. I can relate this event only because the statute of limitations has expired. Seems like the flight crew, who made this flight every other month, took advantage of their location to swap cases of Coors beer for crates of Maine lobster, and distributing the contents of the crates with no profit, as it was a one-item for one-item swap to friends back in Southern California. This time, the crates had a brief appointment for a cooler at the Air Force officers club for a few days before departure.

Spending the night at the Air Force Base, we loaded up aboard the aircraft before daybreak with crew, my detail, and the lobsters prepared for take-off back to California and home. We strapped in, stretched out, roared down the runway and lifted off into the dark morning air. Then, something went—BANG! The crew-chief, who had been up by the pilot, co-pilot and navigator-radioman, dropped down to the cargo deck and shouted, "We're going in!!! Prepare for impact!!!" As he began to quickly strap in. Needless to say, he got our full attention. Before we could react, we felt the aircraft bank hard, straighten out, and hit the ground hard. Fortunately, the "ground" was the runway. We had lost two engines on the same side of the aircraft. Fortunately, we had a damn good pilot. I can't remember that red-headed captain's name.

Good news is we were fine. Bad news, we were going to be at Pease Air Force Base until two engines could be flown in, installed, and tested. Essentially, it was a controlled crash. We hit that runway pretty hard. It took four days, six counting the flight up and the flight back. The pilot called El Toro, and asked El Toro to call Camp Pendleton. Lyn was called by my Regimental Headquarters later in the day saying first, that I was alright, not injured, and second, that I would not be home for a few days, giving her some of the details of the incident. They also called my Gunnery Sergeants wife to let her know. The other seven Marines were not married, so their commander was informed. Later, Lyn told me that is when she began to realize the other side of military life. It could be dangerous. "I began to adjust to that fact," she would tell me much later.

. . .

Around mid-1967, I received orders to Fleet Marine Forces Pacific (FMF Pac, Ground). In other words, to the war in Vietnam. By August, reporting to Staging Battalion for pre deployment combat training, I found myself assigned as an Officer-In-Charge of a Replacement Draft of near ninety or so enlisted Marines. It was seldom when I could get home and I was training on the same base as my home. Another shoe dropped about this time. We were notified, in writing, when I deployed toward Vietnam, Lyn would have thirty-days to vacate quarters. So much for living in government quarters. If we were off-base, she could stay. We were on base. She had to leave. Lyn made it clear to me that there was no way she was going back to her parents. Ever! Under no condition.

Before we vacated our quarters aboard base, the lieutenant who, with his wife, lived next door to us was killed in Vietnam. His wife was devastated. She was in the process of moving off base and now facing the death of her husband who had departed for Vietnam only a couple of weeks earlier. Lyn was especially affected. She comforted the wife of the Marine as best she could, then she scheduled visits to several nearby attractions with all of us in tow, carrying Karen with our other two kids holding each other's hands, while she took dozens of "just in case" photographs. Somehow, not only was luck with us, Lyn kept my morale up. She would care for the home-front while I performed whatever duties and responsibilities the Corps handed me. We gave our friend next door what comfort we could as we vacated the on base residence to move to Oceanside.

We had found a new house for sale right outside the back gate of the base, got a quick VA home loan for the $17,500.00 cost of the newly constructed house, and got her and our three small children into the barely finished home just in time, leaving her to unpack, put a yard in and maintain the household, alone, as I departed for Hawaii, Okinawa, and Vietnam. Lyn, accompanied by our three children drove me to my departure point in front of my replacement draft barracks, and as busses were being loaded, we kissed, said our "see you later" departure message for goodbye, and I boarded the last bus. She later told me she had to sit in the car for a long time before she could drive home. It was the middle of the night.

She had two kids in grade school. And, there was Karen at home with two or three weekly medical and social services appointments in various locations. We had some help. One of my senior NCOs at the brig, John Tolliver, his wife taught school where our kids attended, sometimes she assisted; and, the wife of a warrant officer at the brig offered to keep our three kids while Lyn departed to Hawaii for a rendezvous with me for my Rest and Rehabilitation (R&R) from the war zone in Vietnam. Actually, Lyn needed that R&R more than me.

Several events while I was deployed reveals the character, grit, determination, and pure spunk of my Marine Wife, Lyn. She took the kids to the church we attended every Sunday. As time passed, she felt more and more uncomfortable of the tone of the sermons. One particular day, one particular sermon was accusing US military personnel of purposely killing women and children in Vietnam. When she heard the statement, "Any of our men serving in Vietnam have probably killed women and kids," that did it! Right in the middle of that sermon, she got up from the pew, picked Karen up in one arm, took the other two by a hand each, and walked out of that church in front of a starring, disbelieving, gawking congregation. That took "balls!"

Adding to Lyn's situation at home, the IRS audited our tax return while I was in Vietnam. After the audit, the IRS had to pay an additional return with a check in the mail a few weeks later. She showed them! To help with expenses, Lyn got a job selling jewelry at a jewelry store, after the manager discovered her husband was in Vietnam, *because* he was a Marine serving in the war in Vietnam, he fired her. Another not so small accomplishment she completed was to add a completed concrete patio behind our new house. She noticed concrete trucks coming and going on a daily basis. They were still constructing homes in the neighborhood. She noticed the trucks would use a vacant field to discharge the remaining small amount of concrete mixture and wash out the rotating container. She talked drivers into dropping the mixture into a wood frame she had constructed outlining where she wanted a concrete patio in our back yard. In just a day or two she had soaked and spread enough cement to have a concrete patio. Pretty smooth too. It was a sizable patio which cost—zero.

One of the things I remember most about Lyn being home in Oceanside, California while I was in Vietnam was a conversation we had while packing for our next move which was back to Parris Island. I had returned home from Vietnam just a few days earlier. We were pretty busy because we were actually packing to be transferred to Parris Island rather quickly. She was unaware we had to move before I returned home. I had told her before leaving Vietnam for Okinawa, we would be stationed right where we lived at Camp Pendleton. So, it was unexpected news to her.

We were taking a break from packing, sitting together having a beer. Now, I'm writing this while relying on memories over fifty-years-old. Also, twice I have written about her experiences, while I was in Vietnam, in different format and context through the years. It may not have come out with these exact phrases, but pretty close. The gist will be perfectly clear.

I had casually asked. "Honey, what was your most difficult time while I was gone?" I fully expected her to relate most anything but what she said.

She took a long swig of her beer, looked away toward the front window facing the street, and began to talk: "It's a quiet day. You get up, get the kids dressed and off to school. Pour your second cup of coffee. Then, for some reason, you peer out your front window. You suddenly see and immediately recognize the car. Your heart stops. Breathing becomes difficult, the body begins to shake, your knees go weak and a silent prayer passes through trembling lips. Then, the green military sedan passes your house. 'Thank God!' You utter aloud. Although your chest still hurts, you can breathe again. Then you realize that someone else, someone in your neighborhood is going to get the message that you dreaded. It's another *Killed in Action* call, by a Navy chaplain and a grim-faced Marine officer wearing a black armband on a crisp uniform, driving a military sedan."

She took another swallow, looked me straight in the eyes with tears forming in hers, yet maintaining a grim, serious face and continued, "Honey, that scene took place again and again in this community. We're surrounded by Camp Pendleton, but it could have been and probably has been anywhere, around any military base. More likely than not, it's a young girl, 18 or 19 years old, married to a lance corporal, corporal or sergeant who gets to face the officer delivering the message of death. Here, in our neighborhood it has mostly been officers and staff non-commissioned officer wives getting the notice. Hopes, plans and dreams are shattered. Nightmares become real. Lives are changed forever." She paused again. "Thank God your home. I died enough deaths to last a lifetime while you were gone." So said my Marine Wife in response to my question.

By the way, as previously noted, we had a great time on R&R in Hawaii. We just "lived" and never discussed the war.

. . .

As my tour of duty in Vietnam was winding down, I asked for duty at Camp Pendleton, as the location of our home and family was already in Oceanside. It was granted and I notified Lyn we would be stationed at that location. No move was necessary. She was delighted. However, after arriving in Okinawa on the way back to California and my family, my orders were changed to report to Parris Island instead. From the processing turmoil in Okinawa, Lyn wouldn't know this until I arrived home.

When I broke the news to her, her response was, "Well. . ." She paused, looked straight at me, smiled and added, "Guess we better get packing." Somehow, we got everything accomplished, packed up and furniture underway to the east coast from the west coast, everyone crammed into a stuffed-full-of-stuff automobile and away we went cross-country to Parris Island. I was assigned as the brig officer. Although that particular position rated on base quarters for the person occupying it, none were available at arrival; therefore, we rented an apartment in Port Royal, across the river near Beaufort.

Karen was now four, almost five-years-old. Lyn had borne the responsibility for caring for Karen during my deployment to Vietnam. I tried to pick up the slack by sharing responsibility. But I also had a brig with military prisoners and a staff to manage. Because we were to ultimately live on base, our kids were enrolled in school on base. It was, like Okinawa would be later, a Department of Defense (DOD) school. Every Wednesday morning, the Parris Island Marine band marched to the front of the Depot Headquarters and performed during a formal changing of the guard ceremony by the military police and, weather permitting, the holiday (big) flag was raised at 0800 while the entire student body, teachers and staff from the DOD grade school across the street, weather permitting, stood outside and observed. The little school kids stood and delivered various renditions of a hand-salute during the playing of our National Anthem. Such conduct by school children has been lost in today's complex society. By the start of school year, we were in on base housing.

Karen spent most night-time activities awake, roaming around our Port Royal apartment. We had her sleep in a high-sided baby crib, and double-locked the one apartment front door with a knob-lock, a dead-bolt and a chain-lock. She could get out of the crib sometimes and when we would awaken, we'd just place her back inside her crib, get back in bed trying to get some much-needed sleep. Lyn had been living like that for some time while I was deployed.

One night, about two or three o'clock in the morning, the manager of the apartment complex was knocking loudly on our wide-open door with a soaking wet Karen in his arms. She has gotten out of her high-backed bed, moved a kitchen chair next to the front door, unlocked the knob and dead-bolt, reached up from standing in the chair to unfastened the chain lock and exited our apartment. The manager happened to be mixing chemicals in the pool area when he heard a splash. He turned and saw Karen in the water. As we dried Karen off, profusely thanking the manager, Lyn remarked, "We can't just wait. We must do something!" Of course, she was right.

When I reported the event to my command, there was a flurry of activity, fast enough and in no particular sequence, that made our heads swirl. The next day I reported to my battalion commander, who sent me to G-1 (Administration) at Depot Headquarters to draft an Administrative Action Form, a request for assistance sent to Headquarters Marine Corps. It explained our situation and requested an early transfer to the Southern California areas, which was in the search-pattern area of attempting to locate a facility or anything for Karen. The request form was endorsed by my battalion commander Colonel Doug Bangert, and the commanding general, if I remember correctly, it was General Oscar Peatross.

Interestingly, I received my Navy Commendation Medal with a Combat V for service in Vietnam, at a recruit graduation parade, and was promoted to captain almost at the same time. After my promotion, days later, I was assigned to field-grade (Majorss, Lieutenant Colonels and Colonels) quarters aboard Parris Island. The quarters were big, three-story, wood framed houses, with a wrap-around porch, French doored—huge homes with huge rooms built in 1917. We had to go out and purchase additional furniture from Stucky Brothers Furniture Store at Laurel Bay (again) just to fill in the empty spaces. There was an echo in every room.

A week or so later Colonel Archie Van Winkle, Medal of Honor recipient, Head of the new Security and Law Enforcement Branch at Headquarters Marine Corps arrived to "inspect" the brig. He had dinner at our quarters with Lyn, myself and our kids. We had a nice visit. He had a nice meal. It was the beginning of a long relationship which actually began when I was in Vietnam and responded to a Marine Corps wide request from him for suggestions to assist him in establishing the new Security and Law Enforcement Branch at Headquarters Marine Corps. I had responded, in detail, to his request.

To describe the events during our nine-months at Parris Island, one would get lost in a whirl-wind of activities. I ran the brig receiving accolades, while extensive search queries were dispatched looking for a "Home" for Karen. As usual, Lyn handled everything as she always had, but putting our daughter in a residential treatment facility didn't set well with her. She never voiced it, but it could be "felt."

Finally, a response from a facility at Lakeside, California was received. The Home of Guiding Hands, a Lutheran Church non-profit facility would accept Karen, but only if she could be there within a certain time-frame. Soon!

The ball started rolling for me, in an unsolicited and unusual manner which began with a letter addressed to me from Headquarters Marine Corps. It dealt with a reduction in the number of officers in our Corps. I was a permanent Commissioned Warrant Officer (CWO-2), and a temporary Captain (O-3). In the letter, I was offered three choices: Remain as is, a temporary officer, and take whatever came my way. Or, revert to my permanent rank of CWO-2 and receive in the next promotion cycle a promotion to CWO-3. Or, take a Reserve Commission as a Captain (permanent (O-3), with a guarantee of twenty-years active duty, in short, a Captain USMCR (reserve commission) with a guarantee to stay on active duty until eligible for retirement. After Lyn and I discussed it, I chose the active-duty reserve Captain commission (permanent O-3) guaranteeing twenty-years active duty. Unbeknownst to me, that would remove me from restricted (limited occupational duty) officer status to unrestricted (any occupational duty) status. Therefore, upon acceptance of my choice, we (my family and I) received orders to the 5th Marine Expeditionary Brigade (a combat infantry organization) at Camp Pendleton, California, arriving in time to get Karen into the Home of Guiding Hands. The Marine Corps moves in mysterious ways too.

I reported to 5th Marine Expeditionary Brigade (MEB) Headquarters, who assigned me to Headquarters, 28th Marines (an infantry regiment), as the Commanding Officer of Headquarters Company/Headquarters Commandant, 28th Marine Regiment, stationed at Camp San Mateo on the northern edge of Camp Pendleton. It was a fifty-mile drive from home in Oceanside to my duty location. Like Parris Island, we would be there nine months. The 28th Marines were ultimately redesignated to 3rd Marines. It changed nothing for me. Life as an infantry officer was a life in the field. The war in Vietnam was still hot. Training was intense. Most of the visits to Karen were performed by Lyn.

Once in her many drives to and from San Diego she exited the freeway too late and ran her car into and upon lane divider poles. It wrecked our Nash Rambler vehicle but there were no injuries. Responding to the accident and completing an accident report, plus having Lyn's car towed, a highway-patrol officer picked her and Karen up and, swore he'd get her to her medical appointment on time. He actually ran his patrol car into the loading dock at the hospital, driving too fast and distracted. She could have that effect on people sometimes.

It was, again Archie Van Winkle who ultimately displaced my infantry duties at Camp Pendleton, sending me back to the security and law enforcement field. The Marine Corps had created, or reconstituted, the 5800 MOS for security and law enforcement. Training for Marines entering the new occupational field was to be at Fort Gordon, Georgia, an Army base. We received orders to the US Army Military Police School at Fort Gordon, as an instructor. In this case, it was the first time Lyn did not want to relocate. It would put us on the east coast with Karen on the west coast. We had been through a whirlwind of permanent change of station orders: from Vietnam to Parris Island, to Camp Pendleton, to Fort Gordon in the span of eighteen months. But, the duty at Fort Gordon, with Karen properly placed in an outstanding facility, allowed my Marine Wife, Lyn to begin to excel. She was very popular at Fort Gordon and participated in numerous events, social and professional.

They didn't have a "Marine" uniform, so they dressed Lyn in a sailor costume for a social event at the Officers Club aboard the USS USAMPS, or US Army Military Police School boat.

She missed our daughter, Karen very much and although she got Delta Airlines to fly Karen to Augusta, Georgia for our first Christmas, by that action, she set back all the advances the staff at the Home had accomplished with Karen. Bringing Karen to our home from her home was counter-productive. A bad idea. It was a valuable, hard-learned lesson. But it was a lesson learned! And, accepted!

• • •

Lyn and I have always looked back at two particular duty stations with the fondest of memories: Fort Gordon and the two Okinawa tours of duty (twice accompanied with family). At Fort Gordon she was in her element. It began with the way the Army accepted our Marines and families. We were accepted into everything. Lyn was into the Military Police Officers Wives group and into the Fort Gordon Officers Wives Club. We made friends, some became lifelong friends. When we later departed Fort Gordon and relocated to Okinawa for our first accompanied tour there, many of our Army friends we had met in Georgia were with us on Okinawa during that particular tour.

We had our Marine Corps Birthday celebrations aboard Fort Gordon with the assistance and insistence of the US Army. Archie Van Winkle was our first guest speaker at our ball attended by as many Army personnel as Marines. Lyn, along with other wives began to model clothing for local department stores, take Ikebana courses, began art classes, and create many social gatherings. We had a great time, professionally and socially during that time with the Army. Lyn was actually in a couple of real professionally created fashion shows as a fashion model.

Lyn, the "fashion model" Augusta, Georgia, 1972

Our last Marine Corps Birthday with the Army was in 1972, and it was a bit more low-keyed. After the formalities were conducted, all Marine officer students were invited to our home for a self-help late dinner (Lyn called it an early breakfast), as the formal ceremonies subsided. One of the guests at our home was a student at the M.P. School. A marine captain, let's call him a (pause), no, let's just call him what he was, a marine, with <u>a small m</u>; however, remember the character. Remember the little m! Early on, when I was stationed at the Military Police School, he had asked me via a phone call to assist him getting into our Officers Correctional Administration Course. I did, and later assisted him to get into the M.P. Officers Advanced Course, which I did. He would eventually *pay me back*.

We developed pretty close friendships with Claude and Elizabeth Owen, my immediate boss, and a Marine Corporal at one time in his much earlier life, followed by being a Los Angeles police officer prior to entering the US Army. We got together often for cards, eating out, or boating. Claude had a boat. The four of us and our kids attended the American Correctional Association Conference in Miami Beach, Florida. Had a great time together. We visited Claude and Elizabeth several times in California and when they were in Aruba.

We had two-and-a half-years stationed at that Army Base, and in our final year, the new Fort Gordon Post Commanding General disallowed the annual, and highly successful, Las Vegas night fundraiser for local charities, so the Fort Gordon Army Wives Club asked Lyn to chair the next fundraiser with the caveat, no gambling! No Las Vegas night! Lyn organized and conducted an auction. Not a regular auction either. It was an auction of all auctions.

She worked long and hard hours managing to set-up an auction that gave the local charities a windfall of additional income from the Fort Gordon Officers Wives Club. In addition to garnering numerous high-value, and/or unusual prizes from the local merchants, she got the *undefeated* Miami Dolphins entire team (except Mercury Morris who was in a hospital from injuries) to autograph a football and helmet; a real football and a real football helmet, got

Joe Namath to autograph a jock-strap (don't ask), Burt Reynolds to auto-graph the *Cosmopolitan* nude centerfold (don't even think of asking), Ar-nold Palmer's autographed a golf glove, and so on. Also, since President Richard Nixon had recently returned from his groundbreaking trip to China, Lyn found a way to obtain several copies of The *Little Red Book* (Quotes From Chairman Mao) and several, first-revealed, photos of the Nixon's in China with assistance from an Air Force person by the name of Redmond, if memory serves me correctly. These were also auctioned off. I really don't know how she did it. But, she did.

It was a huge success. That auction was conducted just a couple of days before we departed for Okinawa on an accompanied (with family) tour of duty. After the auction, the next few days were composed of a whirlwind of getting our automobile to the Port of Charleston for transportation to Okinawa, pack-ing, storing most of our household goods and loading our small 800 pounds (two big boxes) of personal items for transfer to Okinawa, followed by packing of eight suitcases for the four of us to carry on the many flights to eventually land in Okinawa.

The Army Post Commanding General sent a formal *Certificate of Appre-ciation* for Lyn to the commanding general of the Marine base in Okinawa, it was presented, along with a scrapbook organized and compiled by the Fort Gordon Officers Wives Club of the Auction Day Fundraising Event, to Lyn by Brigadier General Leonard Fribourg, the Commander of Marine Corps Base, Camp Butler Okinawa. It made Lyn's day. After that clandestinely ar-ranged presentation to Lyn, another surprise evolved from that event. General Fribourg presented me with The Army Commendation Medal and Certificate. Evidently, not only did Lyn and I enjoy Fort Gordon, Fort Gordon must have enjoyed us.

Lyn and BG Len Fribourg USMC

· · ·

The Bates family departed Augusta Georgia's airport in a snowstorm, on a cold February day in 1973. We had vacated our rental home off Tobacco Road, yes, that Erskine Caldwell's *Tobacco Road*, flying to San Francisco, California via Atlanta. Arriving in San Francisco, we obtained a motel for a couple of days to see the sights of the city and ride their famous cable-cars. It was fun, and cold. Eventually, we took a bus north to Travis Air Force Base and from the gate of the airbase, were driven to Officers Temporary Quarters type accommodations to await our flight to Okinawa via Hawaii.

BACKGROUND

Okinawa is an island in the Northern Pacific Ocean which had been occupied by Japan for hundreds of years. It was the location of the last major land campaign of World War II. A study of history reveals it to be the largest amphibious operation ever conducted in the annals of amphibious warfare. It was a combined operation of American Army, Navy, Coast Guard, and Marine Corps combat units against the last stand of Imperial Japan wherein the Navy suffered more causalities than any other service due to the introduction of the suicide aircraft (Kamikaze) of Japan. American forces captured the island and occupied it as an American possession until 1973, the year Lyn and I, along with two of our children arrived on Okinawa. It was returned to Japanese control gradually.

Arriving on Okinawa at Kadena Air Force Base, we were met and driven to temporary housing (family quarters) at a place called Top-of-the-Rock. Our first meal was at the US Army Officers Club located nearby. They actually had a four, or five-piece orchestra playing in the dining room. The Army lived well. We would also discover that we were on Temporary Lodging Allowance (TLA) for ninety-days, which essentially paid for lodging, meals, transportation, even dry cleaning and laundry. We found accommodations in the local community by "house-sitting" for absent owner-occupants, and ate some fabulous meals.

As we were arriving on Okinawa, our appointed sponsors were Major Jim McDonough and his wife Muriel. They became life-long friends. Muriel worked as a volunteer at the Marine Wives Gift Shop on Okinawa, and she worked for a small magazine called *This Week of Okinawa*. It didn't take Lyn too long (I believe the second day after arrival on Okinawa) to begin volunteering at the Marine Wives Gift Shop, located at Camp Hague ultimately leading toward her being asked to be the jewelry buyer for the shop. Twice a year she and another volunteer wife would depart Okinawa for a buying trip to Hong Kong, Bangkok, Manila, Taipei, and other locations. Lyn purchased jewelry, while the other buyer purchased other items to be sold in the Gift Shop. They would be treated royally by merchants, taken to lunch, dinners, and excursions. For Lyn, the jewelry buyer, Raymond Ko, Fred Houseman of Manchu Gems, Peter Pan (real name) from Bangkok Gems, etc., etc... became her contacts, and escorts around their sphere of influence. Lyn got inside the men-only Press Club in Hong Kong, attended ballets, plays, etc. You get the picture.

Husbands were prohibited from accompanying the buyers. We were allowed to join them, *after* the buying was complete. However, on one such buying trip, after the business was conducted and husbands joined wives. Donna's (the non-jewelry buyer) husband Mac, and Lyn's husband, yours truly, were invited for a cruise aboard Manchu II, a motorized, up-scale Chinese junk, by Fred and Bernie Houseman, the owners of Manchu Gems in Hong Kong. Fred and Bernie, his wife, had dual citizenship, actually tertiary citizenship of Hong Kong, Great Brittan, and United States. Bernie, each time she was to deliver the next child, flew to Hawaii where the baby would have US citizenship. The rich live well. It was some cruise, with a captain and crew, a chef, and servers cruising through Repulse Bay and all over the harbor. We saw how *the other-half* lived. A once in a lifetime cruise.

These buyers purchased hundreds of thousands of dollars in merchandise to be sold by the gift shop to American civilians (DOD and private), military personnel and their dependents stationed on or passing through Okinawa. As far as I am aware, that gift shop still flourishes on the Island of Okinawa. It's the perfect place for a young serviceperson to acquire a gift for a loved one back home or accompanying them on "The Rock," at a reasonable price, for quality merchandise.

In addition, Lyn began working for the University of Hawaii (overseas) program, and later began to be the Okinawa Area Coordinator for Pepperdine University's Overseas Graduate Program. She met visiting professors, got them transportation and billeting accommodations, acquired and set-up classroom space and proctored graduate exams for the Master's Program. She once became part of Dale Dye's "What's Happening on Okinawa" Far East Television Network program. CWO Dale Dye was the Assistant Public Affairs Officer for the Marine Base. Currently, you see him in various action type and military oriented Hollywood films.

To me, one of the most unnoticeable positive traits about Lyn occurred as we were serving our first accompanied tour, was how, especially at the Iha Castle (a bachelors officer's quarters with a ballroom and kitchen) facility, which was previously a Continental Airlines hotel, and the Camp McTureous

Officers Club, she would initiate and engage in conversation with the geographic bachelors every time she had the opportunity. She wasn't flirting, just being nice. Most accompanying wives did not do this. Most were wary of these, *Huns From The North*, as these Fleet Marine Force (combat) Marines were nicknamed mostly by the dominate Army personnel and their wives. The Marines relished the title. I never asked her why she spent some time chatting with these particular Marines. It was just her nature; however, I once overheard her telling her friend Muriel, who was always reluctant to so engage the unaccompanied guys in conversation, that she would have appreciated an American female chatting with her husband as he was on an unaccompanied tour. She was right on target.

Matter of fact, at Camp Courtney there was a group of unaccompanied officers who created a "Dining Around Club." They would verbally contract with an accompanied family living on base. Come to their quarters, bring all the food and drink, prepare a scrumptious meal in the kitchen, serve it, everyone would eat a great meal, the officers would cleanup, sit for a while in the evening watching TV, reading a newspaper, chatting with the kids, or playing with the family dog, and at the proper time, get up, gather their leftovers, bid everyone a goodnight, and depart the home. It was their way of doing something nice for a family and having an evening at *their* home. It was *their* home for just a while. This group was very popular among the accompanied tour families. We had them twice.

Once I asked Lyn, in retrospect, a pretty stupid question, if any guys ever propositioned her. Her response was, "Are you kidding me? With almost twenty-thousand male Marines and sailors? I'd be embarrassed if not a one became suggestive. I think the youngest and lowest rank was a Third-Class Corpsman at the Gift Shop, he was around nineteen-years-old, and the oldest, I definitely remember, was a brigadier general, matter of fact, it was actually in the receiving-line at one of the big social functions at Camp Courtney. He was, (pause) drum-roll, the ADC (assistant division commander) of the 3rd Marine Division. Guess what, babe!"

She gave me a big smile, "Sweetie, I turned 'em all down." "So, that's what you meant when you introduced me to him by stating, 'General, I think it's a good idea that you meet my husband,' that evening in that receiving line. I wondered why he had an embarrassed look on his face."

She smiled her impish smile, "Oh, I hadn't noticed."

Introducing Linda Bates

Our cover girl this week is Linda Bates, wife of Marine Capt. Ralph Bates. They have two children, Debbie, 13 and Stoney, 12. Linda is the jewelry buyer for the Marine Officers' Wives' Gift Shop at Camp Hauge. She is an accomplished artist, and her hobbies include snorkling and shell collecting. The Bates have been on Okinawa for about a year and a half.			(TW Photos)

My Lyn featured on cover and inside of This Week on Okinawa, May 1974

Additionally, as I had previously completed a SCUBA course and was an active diver, Lyn also took and completed a dive (SCUBA) course with the National Association of Underwater Instructors (NAUI) and the Professional Association of Diving Instructors (PADI) dive instructors becoming dual certified (out qualifying me), and began an odyssey of collecting sea-shells and coral from the waters of the Pacific Ocean and South China Sea. All perfectly legal at that time. She was an avid member of the Okinawa (Sea) Shell Club meeting at Tori Station on Okinawa. She was such an avid diver, reef walker, and snorkeler she amassed an amazing collection of sea shells and coral, which she has instructed to be donated to an organization or enterprise that will display them to the public.

Lyn walking the beaches on Okinawa

We traveled everywhere we could get transportation to take us: Philippines, Taiwan, Korea, Japan, Thailand and even got to the Republic of Vietnam during the war. We landed at Tan Son Nhut Air Base on a Space-Available flight from Bangkok to Taipei. We sat on the tarmac loading and unloading troops and equipment long enough for Lyn to say, "I've been to Vietnam."

Living on Okinawa was to lead directly into an interesting life-style. For example, consider this following, recurring event while stationed on, what most then called *The Rock*: "Now hear this: Set Typhoon Condition Four," announced the Far East Network Radio and Television message emanating from our television. Winds were up to one-hundred-ten-miles-per hour sustained and up to one-hundred-thirty-miles-per-hour in gust. Condition four was the highest condition set for typhoons. Condition one – a typhoon is expected in forty-eight hours, two - typhoon winds expected within twenty-four hours, three- typhoon winds of sixty-seven miles per hour has arrived and four was, *hang onto your socks*. Rain was sporadic but heavy. Everything and everyone were told to seek shelter. To disobey this announcement was stupid. Very stupid. The last movement of anything outside was the military police making sure everyone was inside. Then they went inside.

This was a monster moving up from Guam. It would bring severe destructive winds ripping stop signs from metal post and sending them flying as deadly missiles through the air. This typhoon was a slow mover. It would encompass and terrorize our island for hours. We'd lose electrical power, water pressure and, possibly some lives. All aircraft, not in hangers, were flown off the island to safe locations. Ships set sail earlier to calmer waters away from the storm's path. Everything outside had been brought inside or tied down. Forecasters told us that winds would reach up to between one hundred forty and one hundred fifty miles per hour and eight to twelve inches of rain could fall. Once or twice, we had gust up to 170 miles per hour.

Within hours the screaming wind drove the rain sideways. Droplets of water began to form on the inside of the outer vertical walls and actually ran in small rivers down the inside walls onto the linoleum floor now clear of rugs, shoes, magazines or any other personal property. Windows rattled in their frames. It was time for a typhoon-party on our little slice of government housing at Kishaba, Camp Sukiran (later to become Camp Butler), Okinawa.

It was typhoon season on Okinawa. And preparations were completed long before the first strong winds reached our shore. Comfort food was stockpiled. Pies had been fried (that was Lyn's specialty), sandwiches made, beans baked, salad assembled, candles and oil-lamps set in place, steel helmets and flack-jackets, along with flashlights and batteries, were stashed in utility rooms near the back or side door of each house in our cluster. Portable, battery-operated radios were fine tuned. Beer and cans of soft drinks were cooled and wine set in place. A one-inch line (rope) connected the back door of one house to the back door of the one next door. Each end of the line was inserted through a small window and tied around the toilet fixture in the small bathroom of each utility room; in case something was needed that was forgotten in the movement to the designated party house. One simply had to slip on a helmet and flak jacket, hang onto the line and move, carefully and quickly to the next house to retrieve whatever was required. For example, we couldn't find the corkscrew, so house to house movement was required to get this vital item. We had four houses connected to the designated party house in a chain.

Typhoon parties were rather common, somewhat foolish, a little childish, a bit dangerous and a whole lotta fun. Some of these suckers lasted for many, many hours. So, rather than sit in an inside room, listening to the howling wind and mopping up water, literally driven through concrete walls and around window and door frames, we would gather in one house and have a party while we mopped up water. Everybody had their assignment. The reinforced concrete, flat roof houses had withstood typhoons for years. They would withstand this baby.

As five families gathered at 1839 Kishaba Terrace on that June day to ride out the storm in whatever comfort they could manufacture, bathtubs had been filled with water for flushing toilets with a bucket dipped into the tub of water, held above the toilet containing the human waste and poured into the bowl from about three feet above. It's an acquired skill. Only number two was allowed into the toilet. For men, number one had to be directed outside somehow and that somehow was between gusts, usually against a large banyan tree in the side yard.

That tree grew over ten feet each year. Women were allowed to do a number one into the commode but no flushing until offensive odor levels were met.

Containers of water dotted kitchen counter tops for drinking. Beer and soft drinks had been cooled prior to loosing electrical power. Food supplied from all five families covered the tops of tables, the useless stove and the non-water space on counter tops. Teenagers and smaller kids were entertained with books, stories, food and games. Those kids acted like young adults without the slightest hint of fear from the typhoon. They were brave guys. Adults acted like kids. We got to know each other well during typhoons. These were, indeed, foolish, fun-filled, memorable times.

Music played over the radio and periodic announcements came across regarding the progress of the typhoon. Sandwiches, salad, beans and fried pies were consumed. Beer and wine filtered through kidneys and many a tall sea story was told above the howling winds, for many, many hours. Some slept in chairs. A few lay across beds. Others just hunkered down until it was near the end. Then. Suddenly. Hours later it came. The music from the radio stopped. Everyone sat up and stared at the radio. Silence dominated for a few seconds. Then, "Now hear this! All clear! Set condition, all clear." The party was over.

Then there was the infamous toilet paper shortage. The military and ultimately the civil stock of toilet paper simply ran out. It lasted a week to ten days and presented an unusual lifestyle to both the military and indigenous population on the Island. Lyn had her mother mail us several rolls of toilet paper. It's amazing the varied uses paper napkins, and towels have.

After Lyn had taken and completed the scuba diving course, she would join me in several underwater adventures. As mentioned, she became an avid collector of Indio-Pacific Sea shells, coral, and numerous photographs and books of shells. Eventually her shell collection would become the talk of the island community. We still have those items of memories from the sea in our home, and have been and are the centerpiece of attention. As mentioned, one of the last wishes of my Marine wife, was that they be donated to an organization who would appreciate and display them. I am aware of no other personal collection of such a variety of sea shells, coral, and books on the subject of specific Marine-life which may exist anywhere in South Carolina.

Lyn's partial collection of Indio-Pacific Sea Shells
and Coral in a pecan wood and glass lighted cabinet

And, what did I do our first tour on Okinawa? As the assistant, I worked the base brig with John Regal as the brig officer, visited the American service personnel locked up in the Japanese prison in Naha. Did a little diving and traveled with Lyn, occasionally. We did much varied travel, to Hong Kong at Christmas (twice), Thailand, Taiwan, Korea, Philippines, and Japan, just to name some. Another thing I am quite proud of during our first accompanied tour on Okinawa: My educational status moved from a High School GED Equivalent to an Associate's Degree in Police Science from Los Angeles Community College. Even with Lyn assisting me in my studies, it took me two-years of night classes to get that degree. It set me up for our next assignment after Okinawa. It was to be at Camp Pendleton. Then, again, fate intervened!

After receiving my AS Degree in Police Science, our good friend Jim McDonough, the base education officer, encouraged me to apply for the "Boot-Strap," Degree Completion educational program for my bachelor's degree. As usual, Lyn insisted I apply; therefore, knowing what would transpire if I hesitated, I did immediately apply and was accepted. At this point a full blown "Catch-22" came into play.

I entered the zone for consideration for promotion to major. My plans, pending orders, expectations, and all else suddenly came to a halt. Marine Corps policy was, that no one in the zone for promotion could be sent to any advanced educational/training program until and unless they were actually SELECTED for promotion. Problem: The Promotion Board was in session, and perhaps would not adjourn until my selected college entrance deadline had passed. I could not execute my orders to the school, but I still had my original orders to Camp Pendleton. But, if I reported to Camp Pendleton on my orders, I could not receive additional transfer orders to anything anywhere else until I had served at least eighteen months. We were in deep kimchi.

Hearing of my situation, enter my commanding general. If I remember correctly, it was Harold Hatch (but, I'm not sure), anyway I was summoned to his office. We sat together, alone in his office, as he talked in a low voice, almost a whisper. "I don't know what to tell you," he began.

"But if it were me," he continued. "You have orders to Camp Pendleton, right?"

I responded, "Yes, sir!"

Looking me straight in the eyes, he continued, "Hell, I'd execute those orders, if it were me," he whispered.

"But, general, if I report in . . ."

He interrupted me, "Who has said anything about reporting in to Camp Pendleton? I'd get lost, captain. You have a bunch of leave due you, then there's proceed time, travel time, hell, you got a whole long vacation of time. Just get out of here, head for California, but don't go to California. You have your orders to Camp Pendleton, just don't report in unless the Board gets out and you're not selected. Just get outta here and get lost. Don't surface until you get selected, then get a change of orders somewhere and get to your chosen school." He looked straight at me again.

"Now, we never had this conversation, you hear me?"

I whispered, "What conversation, General?"

Lyn and I, with two kids in tow, had movers pack and pick up our furniture and head it toward Camp Pendleton. We vacated quarters, sold two cars, packed suitcases, and boarded commercial flights to Tokyo, where we lingered a few days in a hotel, seeing the sights of the city, going up the revolving needle, visiting shrines and temples and just having fun. Then, onward to Honolulu, aboard a Pan Am 747 Jumbo Jet as the only occupants in the loft. Approaching Hawaii, sunrise was magnificent. Arriving in Hawaii and renting a car, we drove the highway over to the north coast where we obtained Bachelor Officer Quarters (BOQ rooms) at Kaneohe Marine Corps Air Station on the north side of Oahu. By car, we traveled to numerous locations on Oahu, playing the sightseer role. We had made it through almost three weeks basically not being noticed, which would come to an abrupt end.

One morning, while we were at breakfast at the Officers' Club at Kaneohe, two, rather sharp-looking, muscular Marine M.P.s entered the dining room and engaged the Mess Non-commissioned-Officer-in-charge (NCOIC) in conversation. Lyn spoke first. "Those M.P.s are after you," she stated matter of fact.

Responding, I said, "No dear, they wouldn't send MPs after me."

About that time the Mess Sergeant pointed his finger toward our table. The two M.P.s approached, saluted, and asked, "Captain Bates?"

I responded, "Yes."

The senior Marine, a corporal stated, "Sir, you are to accompany us to Headquarters Camp Smith."

I asked, "Do you know why?"

The corporal responded with a straight face, not menacing, just factful. "No, sir, all we were told was to ensure you arrive at the adjutant's office at Camp Smith." He paused briefly, "Now, sir. Our vehicle is outside."

"Drive careful. He's all mine, you know," Lyn stated to the M.P.s.

She patted me on the hand as she said, "See you later, babe!" I departed the dining room followed by two huge Marine military policemen to the bewildered astonished looks of the other patrons, and a smiling, waving Lyn, who quietly mouthed the words, "I told you so!"

At Camp H. M. Smith, the adjutant was an old friend of mine. "Where the hell you been? Everybody in the Pacific has been looking for you. Oh, by the way, congratulations, you gonna be a major unless these two M.P.s know more than I do about you. We're modifying your orders to report to the Houston, Texas Marine Reserve Unit for your attendance at Sam Houston State University at Huntsville, Texas." That said, a flurry of activities erupted!

"I have furniture enroute to Camp Pendleton," I stated.

"Already done," he responded. "It's heading toward Houston now."

Quickly I asked, "What about my orders to Pendleton?"

His one word response, "Canceled."

Finally, I asked, "When can I head out to Houston?"

His response, "How fast can you get to the airport?"

As I was leaving the building for the two M.P.s to take me back to the Air Station, he asked somewhat pointedly, "How come you didn't tell your departing command where you'd be?"

I responded, "You mean they didn't tell you where I was heading? They gave me the change-of-station orders. I was on my way to Camp Pendleton. Just taking my time."

. . .

Lyn, our two kids, and I arrived eventually in Houston where we rented a car, drove up Interstate 45 to Huntsville, checked into a Holiday Inn and drove further north to an American Motors Dealership to pick up our new CJ-6 Jeep we had ordered through the Army Air Force Exchange System while in Okinawa. The next day I drove back to Houston to check in with the Marine Corps Reserve Inspector/Instructor (I&I) Staff.

I had 24 months Independent Duty to attend and graduate from Sam Houston State University (SHSU) with a Bachelor's Degree in Criminology. Lyn decided she would also attend classes at the University. Previously, she had attended classes at Mira Costa Community College in Oceanside, California, while I was in Vietnam. It gave her a much-needed break from attending to Karen. She could attend only because people like Mrs. Tolliver as well as a nearby neighbor would watch Karen while Lyn was in class. During our independent duty time, we enjoyed going to the campus together at SHSU, but eventually we had to purchase another vehicle. Lyn was an excellent Art and Photography student in addition to taking standard English, Math, etc. subjects. In one semester, she made the Dean's List.

We purchased a home in the community and made lots of friends. Jack and Margie Westbrook, became very close friends. He was an English professor and a close-by neighbor. We also had young students as friends. We traveled to San Antonio to visit old, Fort Gordon, friends and buddies, took mini-vacations, including driving into Mexico from San Antonio, attended a Texas A&M football game at College Station, watched the famous Texas Prison Rodeo in Huntsville, and just lived the life of college students, plus I made sure I kept in shape physically in preparation and anticipation of getting back to our Marine Corps. Somehow, I managed to run up to ten miles on many days on a side-road parallel to and alongside I-45.

During our first winter, the Marine I&I, a Captain, invited Lyn and me down to the Reserve Unit. My promotion papers had arrived. I was promoted by a colonel who drove down from Dallas. Lyn assisted the colonel in pinning on the oak leaves. Then, came the congratulatory kiss. For that, the colonel did not assist. Our second Marine Corps Birthday while in Huntsville, was in Houston at the invitation of an old Marine Corps buddy, Marine Corps Captain Joe Biggers. He was OIC of an (Navy) NROTC Program. It was an excellent Marine Corps Birthday, our first in a civilian community.

Lyn and the colonel from Dallas make my promotion to major legal

BACKGROUND

Huntsville, Texas is a college/prison town. Located on I-45 just north of Houston, it is one of those towns where everyone knows everybody. I was known as "the federal feller." Living in a community called Normal Park, so named after the original Sam Houston Normal School which became Sam Houston State University, we associated with many professors and students from the University. We enjoyed our time in Huntsville.

As graduation neared, and receiving word that my next tour of duty was to be an UNACCOMPANIED twelve-month tour of duty on Okinawa, we knew we had to prepare for that fact. Not great news, but orders are orders. That's life in the military and naval service. Lyn decided she wanted to live in California around places and people she knew. Our sponsors, when we first arrived on Okinawa for our first tour, were Jim and Muriel McDonough. Muriel was now a real-estate sales person in Carlsbad, California, so Lyn and I drove to Carlsbad, got with Muriel and bought a house in Carlsbad. All in five or six days.

As graduation was upon us, our orders arrived, furniture packed and dispatched, we packed up two vehicles in preparation for departure. Graduation came, and the next day we pointed our cars west and retraced the route Lyn and I had taken two weeks earlier. As usual, again, I left Lyn with unpacking at our new home on Hillside Drive in Carlsbad, California. Sometime in early June 1977, I flew out to Okinawa. They indicated they needed me right away.

Unaccompanied tours of duty overseas, as your family remains stateside, was one of the harder things about being a Marine. In our days, wives could join their Marine husband briefly. Very briefly. If he didn't try to hide the fact his wife was with him, yet remained low keyed, she could stretch the visit out for a few extra days; however, if he squired her around the clubs and social scenes, and his command became aware of the "extra days" situation. Well, "Katie bar the door!" If a wife remained in-country with her unaccompanied spouse more than two weeks, "counseling" developed and could escalate to rather severe, let's call 'em "sanctions." Frankly, the Corps lost many fine people due to its rules on unaccompanied deployments. They came up frequently. But it had a basis in readiness. And, it was logical.

Not being hampered (my word) with families next to them, Marines were ready to deploy and meet foes on an instant's notice. Anytime. Anywhere. They are, indeed, America's 911 force-in-readiness. So, the unaccompanied tour was just a part of what you periodically had to do as a Marine. It was a fact of life. However, my last unaccompanied tour had an interesting and unusual outcome for me and for Lyn. As a matter of fact, it's one of my fondest memories of our time in our Corps of Marines.

A happening I never thought possible, did happen. My family and I had completed a thirty-month *accompanied* tour on Okinawa prior to me attending Sam Houston State University to get my degree in criminology. That first accompanied tour was, in a word, fantastic. Few Marines had the pleasure of bringing their family with them for a tour of duty with a Marine Corps Base overseas in a foreign country. I had been one of them and my family loved it. Now, the hard part, leaving my family in California and deploying for twelve, actually thirteen months, unaccompanied. Geographic bachelors, we called ourselves. Back to Okinawa. Alone! Headquarters Marine Corps said, "They need you." So, I deployed to Okinawa straight away.

. . .

I possessed a military police officer (5803), and criminal investigations officer (5805), military occupational specialties (MOS) and also possessed an infantry officer (0302) MOS. However, quite often the Marine Corps considered that all Marines had only one military occupational specialty—that of *Marine*. After a long flight from San Diego to Okinawa, I reported in to the adjutant of the Marine Corps Base, Camp Butler. The adjutant looked my orders over making this statement. "We don't need another field grade military police officer right now." Pausing, he mused, "Let me talk to the 'Chief'." He disappeared into the Chief of Staff's office and emerged a minute later.

I watched the colonel briefly waved at me as he emerged from his office and entered, what I assumed to be the commanding general's office, and then return to his office, turned, and motioned for me to accompany him into his office. I followed him in. "Ralph, or do they call you Stoney? Good to meet you." We shook hands and he motioned for me to seat myself. "Looks like headquarters messed up. We don't need an M.P. major right now. I'm sending you to Camp Fuji in Japan. You're going to be the executive officer at that camp." I was perplexed but not surprised. Often the Marine Corps moves in mysterious ways. They send me off to Sam Houston State University for two years to get a bachelor's degree in criminology and now, rather than use my new educational foundation in law enforcement, criminal investigations, or corrections, they assign me to assist in running a training base far up north in Japan.

"Who do I report to, Sir?" I asked.

"Stan Tribe. The C.O. of Camp Fuji," he responded. Thus started my contact with two Stan's. Stan Tribe, the then current commanding officer of Camp Fuji in Japan, and Stan Wawrzyniak, the then current provost marshal of the Marine Base, Camp Butler, Okinawa. Two of the finest Marines I've ever worked for. My unusual unaccompanied tour, was beginning, consisting of unexpected twist and turns. And, this was simply the beginning. This tour of duty was going to be quite a surprise, several very pleasant surprises.

I flew Japan Airlines from Naha, Okinawa to Tokyo, Japan and was met at the airport by Captain John Clancy, the operations officer at Camp Fuji, with his van which he called "mouse." We had a long, seemingly uphill drive from crowded Tokyo to spacious Camp Fuji, through a quaint town called Gotemba, Japan. The air was cool and crisp in Gotemba even though it was June. Camp Fuji was another five miles up from Gotemba and located across the street from the Takagahara, Japanese Self Defense Force Garrison. As the executive officer of Camp Fuji, I would be the liaison with the Japanese Self Defense Force (JSDF) at Takagahara and liaison with the Japanese National Police (JNP) in Gotemba and Numazu. Numazu, a coastal port city on the Izu peninsula, was where Marine amphibious units came ashore for training at Camp Fuji and where they departed rejoining the 7th Fleet once training was completed. They came by sea and departed by sea. Getting them to and from Fuji was my responsibility.

I met Colonel Stanley Tribe, my commanding officer. He was a pleasant, professional man. He was on his "twilight cruise," which is that last tour of duty before retiring from the Corps. Although he was on an unaccompanied tour, he, on his own expense and time, brought his wife and two young boys with him to Camp Fuji and had a house he had rented in Gotemba. He explained his rationale to me in this manner: He was fed-up with unaccompanied tours and wasn't going to let his last one be without his family. He had been the last commanding officer of Marine Barracks Philadelphia before it was closed and was destined for retirement after this, his last tour, giving him thirty-something-years active duty. He was shocked when he was ordered to an unaccompanied tour of duty. Without batting an eye-lash, he executed his orders alone, and once settled, sent for his wife and children to join him.

Although I was the executive officer (XO), second in command, he told me that at 1700 (5 p.m.) he was "off duty" and I had the camp on my own. Don't get me wrong. He was a fine Marine. He was a perfect commanding officer. It was simply that, at this late time in his long career, his family had equal status with his Marine Corps duties. I understood that and I respected that. I would cross that bridge four years later.

My office, next to Stan's, was inside an old wooden building near the main gate. I lived a few yards away in a somewhat spacious wooden hut with a living room and a bedroom. It had a TV, receiving only Japanese channels, a couch, easy-chair, tables and a left behind bar that some previous XO had built. The bedroom had a large double bed, a large clothing chest and a large picture-window behind the bed that provided a perfect view of Mount Fuji. On a good day! Built into the bedroom was a metal walled shower. It was comfortable in furnishing and climate. At 5,000 feet up Mount Fuji-yama, air conditioning was not a requirement; but in the winter, soon to come, heat was of utmost importance.

My workday started about six in the morning. Stan got in about seven. I worked until about six in the evening. Stan would leave between five and six, and would take the weekends off, unless I needed him to come in. I worked seven days a week. We had six officers, nine staff-non-commissioned-officers, and one-hundred and seven enlisted men as a permanent staff. With this staff organization we maintained the camp, fixed or replaced anything broken, maintained five vehicles and a platoon of tanks, garnered and maintained good relations with the Japanese Self Defense Force (JSDF), and ensured Marine Amphibious Units were housed, fed, looked after, and received the required training, in addition to getting them from the sea, back to the sea at the conclusion of training.

Disciplinary problems were from rare to non-existent. Safety was of paramount concern. When I arrived Quonset huts used for housing the six to seven-hundred Fleet Marine Force Marines and Sailors in for training every quarter, and the Camp Fuji staff, were heated with fuel-oil fired heaters to heat the quarters. Stan had me change the oil-fired stoves to propane fired heaters. Better heat. Better safety. We also moved the fuel dump consisting of liquid fuel bladders for the platoon of tanks and other vehicles we had assigned to us, from the top of the camp to the bottom of the camp. Gas flows downhill. It was a safety issue. If the bladders ever ruptured, the gas would now not flow through the camp.

In my off-duty time, I ran distances quite a bit. At first, running was difficult due to the altitude being about a mile high. But I got better as time went by. Running through a forest of cedar trees was refreshing. They went for miles. Relations with the Japanese was very good. We were invited to many functions. Military and civilian. We had a MARRS (Military Affiliate Radio Relay Station) facility at the camp. So, I could place a radio-telephone call to Lyn, my wife, in California and she could also call me from the MARRS located at Camp Pendleton. All she had to do was to call the Camp Pendleton MARRS station from home and bingo, we're talking to each other. We kept in touch at least twice a week. It was great to actually talk to each other. Made the time go by better and quicker. It was like a telephone call but you had to remember to say "OVER" when you completed your statement so the radio operators could switch the transmission direction. It was a great benefit.

One day Lyn placed a call to me and placed our daughter, Deborah on the phone. Now remember, every radio operator from Camp Pendleton to

Camp Fuji, and all in between is listening to the conversation. My daughter had a dog named Shasta. She blurted out to me, "Dad. Shasta's in heat. Over."

I started to respond when I heard the voice of one of the MARRS operators, "Over here, honey, everyone is in heat." There was a burst of laughter all across the Pacific Ocean.

The Operations Officer, a major, of the Japanese garrison across the street invited me to climb Mount Fuji with him. We wanted to see sunrise atop Fuji. We started our climb after duty hours, about six in the evening, and made it to one of the way-stations where we bedded down for the night after a bowl of noodle soup. We were awakened at about three in the morning, given a cup of tea and resumed our climb. The Gotemba Trail is one of about five trails up the mountain. It is also the most difficult to climb. It was raining and we were cold. Very cold. We'd take a step forward and up and slide back a step in the wet volcanic ash called "Fuji soil." It was late. We were tired. It looked like we would not make it to the top for sunrise.

Suddenly, from behind us, on that rainy, cold, narrow trail up Fuji, a small female voice spoke. *Go Men, dozo*, she said. Someone was behind us and we were slowing them down. They wanted to pass us. Excuse us please, she had said. The Japanese Army major and I pressed ourselves against the inner wall of the trail as a man and a woman, looking about eighty years old, passed us speaking in Japanese. *Arigato Goziamus*, or excuse us, was all I understood. The major engaged them in a quick conversation and indicated they were celebrating their fiftieth wedding anniversary by seeing sunrise atop Fuji and we were slowing them down. We looked at each other, laughed and seemingly no longer tired we quickened our pace and made it to the top on time to see sunrise and get our climbing poles, referred to as a *"Fuji Stick"* engraved with "SUNRISE ATOP FUJI." I still have that stick.

It would be impossible for me to remember all the invitations received from the Japanese community. My favorite was the Obon Festival a Buddhist Festival which celebrates a time when the spirits of the deceased are able to return to earth to be with their families. The celebration continues for a week.

Me, dancing the Hokkaido Coal Miners Dance at Obon Festival

It was a great tour of duty at Camp Fuji. At Christmas, it slows down and we give as much leave to the men as we can. I requested from Colonel Tribe to be allowed leave at Christmas to fly to California to be with my family. He granted it.

. . .

Almost reluctantly, after my Christmas leave, I was to depart one of the most scenic locations in the world, one of the best duty assignments I had ever had, in a scenic, exotic location, working with great people, both Japanese and Americans, to duty on Okinawa. The Japanese gave me *"presento"* a brass samurai warrior helmet affixed with deer horns. They called it my *"horny helmet."*

Symbolic of the unaccompanied tour I suppose. It sits on a living room shelf today. I'll always remember Fuji fondly but it was another time at Fuji, another bite of the apple, three months later I'll always remember best.

Christmas away from home is perhaps one of the loneliest times for the unaccompanied Marine, or any military service member separated from family. Thankfully, my Christmas that year was with my family in California. It was short. But it was great. Lyn had done a great job with setting up the house and yard, managing the finances and two teen-aged kids, plus visiting Karen frequently. I always marveled at her single-handed accomplishments in that regard. I was beginning to see that if someone wanted to describe the perfect Marine Corps (or military) wife. It would be Lyn, my bride. Two days crossing the Pacific to get home, five days at home and one day crossing the Pacific to get back to Okinawa is tough on mind and body, but it was worth it.

Upon returning, I reported in at headquarters of Camp Butler, saw the Chief, and was introduced to the commanding general and afterwards, was driven down to the provost marshal's office across from Stillwell Gymnasium. The main Military Police (MP) barracks and the offices were in the same building. Then there were the outlying M.P. Districts, three of them. Ultimately, we'd have four. I reported to Lieutenant Colonel Stanley "Stan" Wawrzyniak, the Provost Marshal. He had a perpetual chew of tobacco that seemed to come out of his mouth only when he saw the general, either in the general's office or in the conference room for staff meetings. He'd leave the chewed lump on the general's secretary's desk. She'd cover it with a tissue, and he'd recover it as he was leaving, tossing the tissue in the trash.

He welcomed me, gave me general instructions and showed me to my office and gave me the keys to my car, an AMC Hornet completely marked and equipped with emergency lights, radio and siren, plus he handed me my M.P. badge and my identification card signed by General Robinson. I was now the deputy provost marshal of Camp Butler, Okinawa, reporting to Stan. The other Stan. It was a large organization. Almost two hundred military police uniformed patrol men and women. Thirty criminal investigators. Over a hundred uniformed Japanese security guards guarding gates, ammunition storage areas and special details, plus a twenty-four person K-9 unit (dog and handler) and a civilian administrative staff. It was the largest military police department in the Marine Corps. I was instantly made busy.

The US Army still had M.P.s on the island but we Marines were taking over their duties. We were growing. We were also planning to change driving from right side drive to left side drive, based on the fact that since 1973, Okinawa had belonged to Japan and they drove on the left. Since 1945, when American military and naval forces captured Okinawa, it was a United States occupied and owned island. We drove on the right. I pitched in and got buried in my work. Lyn and I would talk on the MARRS network about twice a week. Stan was on an accompanied tour with his family. The deputy provost marshal position was technically an accompanied billet, but I was technically on an unaccompanied tour. Stan encouraged me to, "Bring her over for a while." He'd say that often.

Lyn and I talked about it a couple of times and on a cold, rainy day in California and night in Okinawa, while talking on the MARRS network, we both agreed to her flying over to Okinawa for a ten day stay. The kids were older now and Karen was still in a Home in Lakeside, California. So, as it continued to rain and the cold wind blew, she eventually landed in Naha, Okinawa via Tokyo. Bob Dylan was on her flight from California to Japan. She said that that bunch made the flight interesting. I still worked a work-day and we stayed at the guest quarters and went out in the evenings. Of course, Lyn had friends on the island from two years previously, on our first accompanied tour.

We were having breakfast together at Camp Foster Officers Club each day. It remained cold and wet. One day, in the morning, at breakfast, a Navy officer came into breakfast and said it was snowing at the Navy base at White Beach, also on Okinawa. "That does it," I said. "I can't let you come to Okinawa and all our days are rained or snowed out," I said to Lyn.

We went to my office and I placed a phone call to Stan Tribe at Camp Fuji. "Bring 'er up. You got your old hut. Nobody's replaced you yet." That's all I needed to hear. I then went into Stan Wawrzyniak's office.

"Take a week and show her a good time. I need a report on Fuji's security anyway. Bring it back with you." Then he said, with a wink, "Have a good trip." I was going to have a second bite of the apple at Camp Fuji. I really wanted Lyn to see it.

BACKGROUND:

Camp Fuji is the remnants (or remains) of three previously established camps near or on the mountain. North Camp, Middle Camp, and I believe South or East Camp was the third in the days of yore. Today, it is a single, large training camp, part of Camp Butler, maintained by the Marines for training purposes of the Fleet Marine Forces. It is used by both American forces and Japanese forces, sometimes jointly. When I was there it sat in an almost pristine forested area stretching for miles covered by the scent of cedar from thousands of cedar trees in a deep forest. I am so fortunate that Lyn experienced a taste of Fuji and its surrounding wonderland.

Lyn and I flew on Japan Airlines (JAL) from Naha to Tokyo. It was a weather rough flight. They couldn't even hand out the bento-box meal it was so rough. John Clancy picked us up with the mouse and a wool Aran (Irish) sweater, gloves and cap for Lyn. The drive up to Fuji through Gotemba was clear, crisp and colder the higher we got. Gotemba was alive with color. Window boxes displayed colorful cabbage plants in artful design. Airborne food flavor wakened senses as it floated through the crisp air as we passed many restaurants and cafés on the drive up to Fuji.

Lyn met Stan Tribe and instantly liked him. We settled into my old quarters. The two butane heaters made it warm inside. Outside was a crisp, clear minus five degrees. Two or three feet of snow was packed on the ground. But roads and pathways were clear. It was great weather. The entire camp sits on what we called Fuji soil. It's small granules of volcanic ash and crushed up lava rock, and crunches under your feet as one walks on it. We ate breakfast at the mess hall each day. I paid my basic allowance for subsistence (BAS), or money for food, of course and paid the civilian rate for Lyn. The troops liked Lyn. She was especially a hit with the Staff NCOs.

Lyn at Camp Fuji on Lake Yamanaka
Mt. Fuji in background

We'd go, at their invitation, to the small Staff NCO Club after evening meals and interact with them and the one or two officers who would also be present, by invitation. Lyn found out what it was like to have a couple or three drinks at that mile-high altitude inside a warm cozy club with a hot coal-burning fireplace noisily crackling and occasionally emitting whiffs of white smoke from small pieces of green cedarwood catching fire, and then walk out into the cold, thin mile-high air.

On one of our almost every evening invitations, she and a staff sergeant got into a friendly argument about drinking wine. Lyn blurted out that she could drink the staff sergeant, in her words, "under the table." Challenge accepted! While the bartender kept count, they began their self-inspired wine challenge. To make a rather long drinking story a bit shorter, it was not under the table, it was off the barstool. After copious amounts of wine had been measured, poured and consumed, late that night the staff sergeant fell off his barstool while Lyn asked for another glass of wine. Someone assisted the staff sergeant to his quarters.

Lyn finished her last glass of wine in front of her ardent admirers and we began to depart the club. It was somewhere below zero degrees outside, and the slightly falling snow was pretty deep, but packed. I asked Lyn if she required assistance and instantly got several volunteers. She brushed it off, donned her thick Irish sweater, gloves, cap and scarf preparing to walk the sixty to seventy yards to my hootch.

There was a small, curved, Japanese style bridge just outside the club going over a sizable frozen carp pond and that's how far she made it. I grabbed her arm, held it over my shoulder across my neck. With my other hand held around her waist, walked my bride back to our warm accommodations. I managed to get her shoes, hat, sweater, and scarf off and rolled her into the bed. She awakened me just after daybreak. She was up on her knees, looking out the picture window snapping pictures with her camera of the changing scenes of Mount Fujiyama. The staff-sergeant was not present at breakfast that morning.

She loved to wake up in the morning and look out the window at the close-up snow-covered mountain. The mountain, in winter, changes its image every minute or so from blowing snow at the summit. It is an old dormant volcano 12,500 feet in altitude and we were sitting at the 5,000-foot mark. And it's an awe-inspiring sight, especially when up close and personal. The area around Fuji is cold, very cold, in the winter. January through April is the dead of winter.

We drove all over Gotemba, Yamanaka, Numazu and all of James Clavell's—_Shogun_ areas. We had an absolutely fantastic time. Mister Stuart Toshiro, Camp Fuji's Cultural Affairs man, seemed to alert the local eating places as to our presence. Lyn, who is allergic to onion, never had an eating problem. We were treated to some picture-perfect scenes of Japan at a time and place where gawking international tourist were absent.

One brutally cold evening, Stan invited us to his home for dinner. It was a typical Japanese house in a Japanese community. They only heat the room you are currently occupying by transferring the portable heater from one room to another. The dining area contained a short square table sitting over a large square hole in the floor. Inside this square hole, at the bottom, are a couple of five-hundred-watt light-bulbs. Your feet go into this hole and you sit at the table on cushions with a hard, rigid back. It keeps your feet warm. That's the theory.

The longer we sat and ate, the colder Lyn got. After we finished the meal and were having sake, Lyn asked to use the bathroom or _benjo_, as the Japanese call it. She was gone an inordinate length of time. Finally, Stan suggested I go check on her. I found the room and knocked quietly asking, "Lyn! You, Okay?" Her response brought laughter. It seems that the toilet seats in most Japanese homes are heated, for obvious reasons. Lyn said that this was the warmest place in the house and she wasn't sure she could leave that spot. The Tribe's got a kick out of it and it is still funny today.

· · ·

Good things come to an end. I took Lyn to Tokyo for her flight back to San Diego and I then flew back to Okinawa and resumed my duties as deputy provost marshal. It was in mid-April or early May when General Robinson asked me if I would accept another accompanied tour of duty on Okinawa. This tour to be as the provost marshal. He had me call Headquarters Marine Corps and talk to the officer assignment people. I then placed a call to Lyn and asked her if the family wanted another accompanied tour on Okinawa. It was unanimous. In late-April Stan, preparing to retire from the Corps, transferred to

Headquarters Battalion as the commanding officer and I became the Provost Marshal of Marine Corps Base, Camp Butler Okinawa, reporting to General Kenneth Robinson. As far as I know, I'm the only major to occupy the provost marshal billet on Okinawa. My family arrived in June 1978, minus our daughter Deborah who would join us later, for a second bite at the apple, an extremely rare second accompanied tour with the Marine Corps Base on Okinawa. And, the Marine Corps came through again.

General Ken Robinson CG of Camp Butler With inscription to Lyn and me
The caption under the photo reads:
Major Ralph Bates, 1 Sept. 79
As Butler's "Top Cop" you were always "on the scene."
Whether the "scene" was social or professional, Bates made it better! Marie and I
enjoyed our many happy associations with you and Linda. Best wishes. K. Robinson

I received orders to a Provost Marshal Conference at the FBI Academy at Quantico. Then, after my conference at Quantico, in returning to Okinawa, I flew to San Diego where Lyn picked me up. For one of the first times, I helped her pack, sell vehicles, and sell a house before we travelled together, minus Deborah who, as mentioned chose to remain Stateside temporarily and travel on orders to Okinawa to join us later. Actually, Lyn had already accomplished most of the task on her own. She even got the real estate agency to buy back our house we had purchased nine months earlier. We made a $10,000.00 profit with Lyn's abilities at negotiating. She was definitely a perfect Marine Wife, that Lyn.

During this second tour we did all those things that we had done before, on our first tour. Plus, we did those things that we wanted to do on our first tour but never had the time, the money or both to do them all. We traveled to many places like Hong Kong for Christmas, twice. We went to Korea and Taiwan and bought a lot of things, furniture mostly. Most of it was hand-made. We still have most of it. Lyn and daughter Deborah travelling with a neighbor friend, flew on Air Force, Space Available aircraft to the Philippines on a buying trip. In addition to their haul from that trip, we bought many, many items that last tour on Okinawa. And, we continued to dive and snorkel as Lyn added to her massive sea shell collection.

Lyn with scuba tank, and equipment, plus, her underwater hunter instinct

Lyn, shell hunting from Okinawan sampan

Things had changed on Okinawa between our first and second accompanied tour. Just as, for sure, if we went back today, we wouldn't recognize much of it. For us, being there from February 1973, through June 1975, and again from June 1978 through June 1980 our view will always be a little part of America overseas. It was a tight-knit little community. It took a long hard fight for the forces of America's military and naval power to wrestle it away from Imperial Japan. Now it's theirs again. Life moves on. But fond memories of our Okinawa and Camp Fuji experiences will never fade. Never move on. Somehow the second bite of the apple is so much sweeter. We certainly had some experiences. Some were light-hearted, some were not. One of the light-hearted events just kinda snuck up on us. It wasn't planned, it just happened. Let me tell you about that one. Our first and last Navy Birthday Party:

. . .

"Dead Bug!" someone shouted. Immediately all patrons in the bar, some in uniform, others in "civvies," ladies in dresses, and luckier ladies, in pants suits, immediately hopped off bar stools, shoved chairs away from tables and dropped, laid, or otherwise oozed to the floor of the bar room, rolled over onto their backs, lay with arms and legs pointed toward the ceiling, twitching wildly and simulating a dead or dying bug. Last one down, according to the bartender, bought the next round of drinks. It was a game. A game designed to break the rhythm of daily life for hundreds of Marines, and others on Okinawa. Almost all of them were serving a twelve-month tour of duty, unaccompanied by wives or American girlfriends, the geographic bachelors of the Corps. But a few, a very small few, were accompanied by their families for a two-and-a-half-year tour of duty. Doing the dead bug thing was fun. Only one game a night was allowed in any bar. Yes, even this silly game had rules. Such was life on Okinawa in the 1970s. It's been around for a while. Former President George Bush knows from first-hand experience how the game is played from his fighter pilot days around Houston, Texas, but I don't think he does that anymore.

Lyn and I had been living on Okinawa for just over a year on this tour and we had been there before. We had been invited to a dinner-party to celebrate the US Navy's birthday. It was October, 1979. Actually, several of us Marine, accompanied types, had been invited by the Navy captain who ran the US Naval Hospital at Camp Kuwae, Okinawa. It was, as the engraved invitation noted, a formal affair. An Admiral accompanied by his aide, was the honored guest. All the Navy folks were accompanied by their wives or girlfriends. Or both. Our senior Marine in attendance was a colonel, our chief-of-staff for the Marine Base. The various general-staff officers were in attendance, each accompanied by wives. My position as the provost marshal of the base placed my wife and me on the invited guest list. Our general was tied up with a sudden visitor from Japan. It was the American ambassador to Japan, also a Marine, Ambassador Mike Mansfield, so he took precedence, and our general was unable to attend the event. Our colonel stood in for him.

As we mingled and procured cocktails at the bar, we Marines eyed the large seating chart at the dining room entrance. The head table consisted of the admiral and his aide, the captain, two or three commanders, and a scattering of lieutenant commanders, each with wife. The Japanese governor of the prefecture of Okinawa, the Kadena Air Force Base commander and an army lieutenant colonel, each with wife, and also the American Express, Okinawa chief and the Hilton Hotel executive (civilians), each with wife.

A few of us were wondering and voicing aloud why our colonel wasn't at the head table. One of us jokingly suggested that the Navy captain must have read the book *The Great Santini* and didn't want a repeat of the "mushroom soup" scene. That drew a laugh. What didn't draw a laugh was the discovery that all of us Marines and Marine wives were assigned to the same long table off to the side of the dining room. It reminded me of the proverbial Sunday gathering of several families, after church, at Grandma's house and the children always ate at a separate table away from the adults. It caused some conspicuous consternation in our little group.

Our chief-of-staff was a fine Marine. He was, at times, a bit too formal, but he was a patient, cool, confident gentleman. While we were fussing and fuming about the perceived "insult" to our colonel and our Corps in general, with nothing but a smile and nods to the Navy personnel seated and standing between our table and where we had gathered to fume, he led us directly to our assigned area, asked us to be seated and we watched as he approached the admiral and captain. He stuck out his hand and shook hands with both officers, bowed and smiled at their wives, spoke briefly to the officers and wives at the head table, excused himself and returned toward our table. Passing the bar, I noticed he "lifted" a bottle of Jim Beam Kentucky Bourbon.

He returned and promptly poured each of us a shot of booze. He then lifted his glass and announced, just to our table, "To the Navy." and gulped the glass dry.

We all repeated, "To the Navy" and gulped the drink-some faster than others. Lyn got hers down but it took two or three gulps combined with a breathless recovery. The colonel got off a couple of another toasts, to something or another, before dinner, which was accompanied by copious amounts of wine, served by waiters. These waiters were slow in charging wine glasses at our table, so one of us, can't remember who, took a couple of bottles from our guy and we served our own wine. Occasionally we'd toast something or someone. We were perhaps, somewhat rowdy. Some might say.

We were about halfway through our meal, I think, when I saw the admiral dispatch his aide toward our table. The young lieutenant walked directly to our colonel and, rather loudly, (I thought too loudly) said, "You Marines are too loud. You're requested to hold it down."

Whereupon our colonel looked the lieutenant in the eyes and quietly said, "Get lost, Sonny." The aide, looking a bit perplexed, looked over toward the head table, glanced briefly at our smiling faces, and returned to whisper into the admiral's ear.

Our colonel was only halfway through another toast to either the Royal Marines or Ann Margret, one of the two, or both when the admiral suddenly appeared beside him. "Colonel, you Marines are ordered to be quiet or leave." Without missing a beat, the colonel snapped to attention and responded.

"Aye, Aye, Sir."

Whereupon he barked out to our table, "Marines! Marine wives! Attention!" We all, wives included, stood at attention.

Then the colonel said, "On my left," he pointed at the left side of the table, "Right Face!" He then pointed to the right side of the table. "Right side, Left Face!" Then, to the astonishment of the admiral, he announced, "Marines. Marine wives. On my command, reassemble at our club." Then, he commanded, "Forward, March!" We marched in perfect unison out of the Navy birthday party.

My Lyn just had to give out a "ha!" as she marched past the admiral. Someone carried the empty Jim Beam bottle and deposited it in a nearby trash can by the exit.

We reassembled a few minutes later at the Camp Butler Officers Club, up the hill, on the other side of highway 330, near Camp Butler Headquarters. I noticed the lights in the headquarters building were still on. Just a casual observation. The manager-bartender was the only person present in the club. We relayed the story to him and he mixed us "Golden Cadillacs," his specialty drink, to celebrate our being thrown out of the Navy's birthday celebration. His concoction was a mix of several spirits topped off with a large scoop of vanilla ice cream. It was a smooth, powerful mixture. We each had a couple.

A few departed for home but the colonel, five lieutenant colonels and another major and I, along with our wives tried to shut down the club at midnight or just after. As luck would have it, when the manager announced, "That's it, Marines. Closing time! One more round ladies and gentlemen. Who's buying?"

My Marine Wife, Lyn, responded, "We'll see," then loudly proclaimed, in a pretty good rendition of a Marine Drill Instructor, letting out a yell as she was sliding off the bar stool, already half way to the floor, *"Dead Bug!!!"* Eight Marine officers, in full, formal, mess dress uniform and eight wives in formal, long and/or short cocktail dresses, literally flew onto the floor, rolled onto their backs and raised their legs and arms in a violent shaking death pose of a zapped bug. Women were trying desperately, at the same time, to hold their dresses together in some insane sense of modesty. Our bartender was beginning to announce that our colonel was the last down when he suddenly was unusually and unmistakably very quiet.

From my "dead bug" position on the deck, sensing that something had happened to cause the bartender to go instantly quiet, I looked up and directly into the face of our commanding general, Kenneth Robinson and, what I assumed to be a very important person standing next to him. "Good evening, General."

Without missing a beat, the general stated, "Mister Ambassador, this is Major Bates, our provost marshal."

Ambassador Mansfield looked down at me and stated, "Good evening 'top cop.'" Still on my back, I responded as best as I could with a, "Good evening, Mister Ambassador. And, without further comment, the General and Ambassador

Mike Mansfield, a Marine of World War II, then stepped over my prone body to walk over and lean on the bar, engage in quiet conversation and order a brandy night-cap from the recovering bartender. Such was life on the "Rock" for Lyn and me.

. . .

When I was transferred to Camp Butler, Okinawa as deputy provost marshal working for the legendary Stanley J. Wawrzyniak, back in California Lyn was managing a household with two teenaged children, visiting Karen, and using, not passing time as best she could, always busy waiting for my overseas unaccompanied tour of duty to be completed so she could have her husband back. Stan was assigned as provost marshal of Camp Butler, Okinawa. Although Stan was a lieutenant colonel and the provost marshal billet was that of a colonel's rank, his reputation, and brashness solidified his position. Just three months into my assignment, right after my wife paid me a visit from the States, our commanding general, appointed me, a major, as the Provost Marshal of Camp Butler. Stan was assigned as commanding officer of Headquarters Battalion while awaiting orders back to the States and a well-earned retirement.

Now, understand this, I was certainly no Stan Wawrzyniak. I didn't chew tobacco, didn't wear a Navy Cross, wasn't a WW II, Korean War, and Vietnam War combat veteran, didn't have a reputation as a "hell-fighting, devil-may-care Marine," and didn't leave a wet, sloppy "chaw" on the general's secretary's desk each time while visiting the general. Remember, she would cover it with tissue until Stan emerged to retrieve his "chaw" lump." Stan was all that, and more. Yes, I was a far-cry from this legendary Lieutenant Colonel Stan Wawrzyniak. But, suddenly—I am THE Provost Marshal of the largest military police unit in the Marine Corps. I was humbled, awed, and elated at the same time.

Immediately, my big challenge came from "full bird" colonels, as opposed to silver-oak leaf lieutenant colonel's, who apparently felt they should be THE provost marshal, and proceeded in various direct and indirect methods to oust me from my position. I faced those challenges, with a little bit of help from other sources. Let's just say that having strong support from your boss and having excellent relations with the Japanese National Police, plus giving top-notch performance in supporting your boss, gives one a unique advantage.

It was at this juncture that the second accompanied tour on Okinawa developed and ultimately my family joined me. Lyn sometime bristled when she would hear of these developing situations with someone attempting to get me into a position wherein someone else could step into my position. There was talk and Lyn was not hard of hearing. I assured her things were fine. No problems were brewing. None were brewing, in part because my military police and criminal investigators were also top-notch performers.

The general gave me and my department many unique missions. One in particular was to provide security for the extraction of Marine Private First Class, Robert Garwood (the deserter and collaborator) from Vietnam. It was around March 1979, that representatives from the United States Department of State met in the general's office. I was present at that meeting. Seven years after US forces were withdrawn from Vietnam, four years after the fall of the Republic of Vietnam to the Communist, a *captured* Marine wanted to come home.

After that meeting, and understanding my mission, I requested written authorization for the use of deadly force. My general authorized it, in writing. I selected a detail of my men, drew hand-held radios for each, equipped them with shoulder holsters for their assigned .45 auto pistols, trained them in drawing and firing from concealed (under the shirt) positions, outlined a comprehensive security plan consistent with the use of deadly force, selected and "sanitized" a section of the US Naval Hospital where we were going to keep our man, and rehearsed various action and reaction procedures, often with an actual C-130 aircraft. By the time the target (Garwood) would arrive via C-130 from Thailand, we were ready.

Lyn and I were at a party at the general's quarters when I was notified, by the general, of the pending arrival of the C-130 transport aircraft. Mentioning that I'd drop Lyn off at our quarters on my way to the Futema Air Station, the general replied, "Take her with you. It was a no-show." Garwood was not on the aircraft.

It seemed that the wives of some of the general staff were aware of the extraction operation, while Lyn was totally unaware of anything other than I was always armed and always had a hand-held radio. Being the provost marshal she rarely asked questions. She rode with me to meet the aircraft with only the crew, the extraction team and a couple of military lawyers aboard. As everyone disembarked from the aircraft, it was discovered the two lawyers required transportation to their quarters. I took them in tow placing them in the back seat of my marked patrol vehicle. By the time we arrived at the bachelors' officers' quarters, as the two lawyers loudly conversed with each other along the route, Lyn knew all about the operation to extract a suspected military deserter from Vietnam.

After dropping the two lawyers off, she said, "I think I'm the last wife to know about this. Now, I realize what some of the wives were talking about. I had no idea, now I do. But," she finished, "it goes no further than me." She was a true Marine Wife. A rare breed, indeed.

A week later, it all came together. With assistance from the French Ambassador to Vietnam, Garwood was extracted from Vietnam to face a court-martial. We got him from the landing of the aircraft at Futema's airstrip, to Kuwae Naval Hospital, where we kept him with limited access for several days, while he was positively identified via fingerprints and dental records. He was given a physical exam and maintained in total isolation. Then, we set up a ruse to get him from Okinawa into confinement at Great Lakes.

While the world-wide media concentrated on, what they initially thought was the evacuation of the Shah of Iran being conducted, but later discovered it was a Marine deserter from the Vietnam War who had perhaps served in combat <u>with</u> the enemy against Americans, they were in a frenzied drive for information and access. Both were denied. When we were set to move Garwood, they followed our Garwood look-alike decoy, meandering from the hospital to Kadena Air Force Base, while two of my CID men along with an undercover escort, departed for the Naha Airport to board a North-West Orient Airline's flight to Chicago with Garwood in tow and in cuffs. Mission accomplished.

I remembered the Garwood case intimately. As the officer-in-charge of the CID (criminal investigation department) in Vietnam, we had "salt and pepper" reports periodically. That was a black man and a white man, suspected to be Army or Marine, who appeared to be leading attacks against Marine forces in combat. Thus, they were named, "salt and pepper." I am convinced to this day that Garwood was the "salt." He was court martialed at Camp Lejeune.

. . .

Interestingly, about a year after the Garwood event, I inadvertently slid into one of those "valleys" by conducting a rather sensitive investigation at the request of my boss. Without disclosing too much, let us just say that it was a domestic incident type investigation. The investigation was conducted professionally and in a quasi-clandestine manner. I was pleased with the results, and so was my boss. The unexpected problem arose when the commander of one of the two subjects of the investigation felt I had overstepped my bounds. He was NOT pleased with the results of the investigation. My boss was pleased, but this other boss of one of the subjects, was not. It went up the chain-of-command. When I delivered my CID report to him, I took an ass-chewing par-*excellence*! It was the first time I had been in trouble for doing my job.

After that humbling experience, I reported the facts back to my real boss. No sweat! As expected, my boss supported me completely, without any dissention. I was assured: Everything would be fine. Then, the unexpected happened.

As a result of orders from Headquarters Marine Corps, these two commanders changed positions with each other. The "not pleased with the results of the investigation," became my actual boss. Even with the change, I seemed to be still doing fine, when, out-of-the-blue, a report came in that we (the Marines) were missing some M-72 LAAW's, a light anti-tank assault-weapon (a rocket), from an ammo bunker located in one of our camps.

Several separate issues began to merge. First, the International Economic Summit was convening in Tokyo, Japan. Second, the terrorist group, Japanese Red Army, had been active in Japan, and a cadre was supposedly on Okinawa.

Third, President Jimmy Carter was attending the Summit and was airborne on his way to Tokyo. Fourth, a LAAW can take down an aircraft with a lucky shot. Fifth, someone had fired a rocket, believed to be home-made, at the Imperial Palace in Tokyo, and, sixth and last, was the treaty referred to as the Status of Forces Agreement (SOFA) between Japan and the United States; it stipulated that this type of an event <u>must</u> be reported to the Japanese National Police.

I was the one who would normally report this event; however, I was ordered by my new boss, not to report the event. I was in a quandary. The worst-case scenario flashed by my psyche: *US President's aircraft downed by missile approaching landing in Tokyo.* I shook that thought outta my mind only to have it, or something similar reenter, again, and again. *Provost Marshal admits he was aware of Missing Rockets.*

I sought advice from several trusted sources; however, the only sound advice received from other Marines was: "You should ask your boss to put it in writing."

When I tried, that didn't go over very well with my boss! Another piece of *advice* was—"You're in a hell of a mess," and, "Wouldn't want to be in your shoes." I contemplated everything from resigning my commission to defying an order.

Naturally my bride took one look at me when I entered our quarters and immediately asked, "What's wrong, babe?"

I relayed the highlights to her, and her level-headed response was, "Do what's right, hon. Do the right thing."

Then she sat down and asked, "So, he wouldn't put it in writing?"

I responded, "Of course not."

Her response made all the sense in the world. "Then, it's illegal."

Just as I had finished making a decision, and contemplating the end of my Marine Corps career in an inglorious fashion, my interpreter/cultural affairs officer, a civilian Japanese National, entered my office telling me that the Chief of the Prefectural Police was on the phone inquiring about the missing weapons. The Japanese National Police were aware of the incident. And I didn't do it!!

I did find out later that when the weapons were discovered missing, the Japanese security guard assigned to the weapons storage area of the missing weapons, had reported that fact to my Japanese Security Guard Commander. That commander, hearing of my difficult situation, discussed it with the interpreter/cultural affairs person, and he, the Japanese Security Guard Commander had apparently notified the Prefectural (National) Police.

I could feel it when something just ain't right. And, I could *feel* it. So could Lyn. Some of our acquaintances began to have shorter and shorter conversations with us. Some of the general staff officers looked at me as if I was a *dying calf in a hail storm*. The kicker came when I was no longer called upon to comment at the weekly staff meeting. I just sat in the conference room against the bulkhead (wall) and kept my mouth closed.

Wait! It's not over. A few weeks, or maybe it was a couple of months later, a lieutenant colonel reported to Camp Butler, and was assigned to duty as THE Provost Marshal of Camp Butler. I was reassigned as deputy provost marshal. As the new provost marshal was adjusting to the job, my office was moved to the basement of the military police building. I was isolated from the staff of the provost marshal's office. I knew if I remained in that basement office, other *shoes* would start *dropping*.

I went into the office at midnight one night, picked up the phone, and called Security and Law Enforcement Branch at Headquarters Marine Corps. Upon getting access to the Director, Lieutenant Colonel Adolf Sgambelluri, my first words after identifying myself were, "Get me out of here!!" I stated loudly and forcefully to the Head of Security and Law Enforcement.

"Start packing! I'll have your orders cut at once," was the thankful reply.

. . .

The Bates family departed from a much-desired, and much cherished accompanied tour as an appreciative second bite of the apple. This time with a definite feeling that things would never be the same in my Marine Corps career. We did our usual stopover in Hawaii, and proceeded to fly into the Los Angeles

Airport where we were met by two military policemen from the Twenty-Nine-Palms Provost Marshals Office which the provost marshal had dispatched to get us from the airport and into a motel in the, adjacent to the base, town of Twenty-Nine-Palms. It's about a hundred-mile drive from Los Angeles to the base and town. As usual, government quarters were not available so we rented a house month-to-month in town.

The Marine Base and the town are located in the high-desert north of Palm Springs, California. In land mass, it is the largest military base in the United States. Main-side is rather small as the permanent population of Marines, Sailors and our Air Force Veterinarian did not constitute a sizable need. Some schools reside at the base, and now an air component takes up residence there. Desert combat, and combined-arms training takes place out in the desert bowl. It can get hot there. Real hot! What is it (the base) nearby? Nothing! Oh yeah, the town got its first traffic light right before we arrived there. It was the only location wherein Lyn was not pleased to be there, but she ground it out. She even got in a few more college credit-hours at College of the Desert.

Making a long enough story as short as possible, after a brief stint as the Executive Officer of Headquarters Battalion (I was getting used to that pattern), I became the Provost Marshal of the Marine Corps Air-Ground Combat Center, Twenty-Nine Palms, California. The duty was fine except the assets were minimal. Battalions would rotate in for training, have a few days off as "Liberty-Time," and rotate out back to their permanent location. It was that "Liberty-Time," that caused me most of my problems. Being short staffed compounded my problems. However, backing from the commanding general and chief-of-staff was good and consistent. Nevertheless, those damn LAAWs, that basement location, that ass-chewing from a very high ranking officer, and those final days and weeks on the "Rock" bothered me. Lyn could sense it.

After getting assigned base quarters, and attending the Marine Corps Birthday celebration for the M.P.s at the base (since M.P.s were all on duty for the Marine Corps Birthday, we held an earlier, separate Birthday celebration), and later in Palm Springs, where the officers bash was scheduled for the majority of the base officers, my wife and I sat together at our dinner table with my battalion commanding officer, John Caynak and his wife, as my twenty-sixth-year of Marine Corps service was approaching. John was an excellent commanding officer.

We began to have a never-had-before discussion about our future within the ranks of the Marine Corps. As usual there was the typical plus column and the minus column on the paper tablet before us on the table. Clearly the various incidences as Provost Marshal confronting seniors, the LAAW incident, and the "domestic" event, my hasty departure from the basement in Okinawa, and even my Criminal Investigation Officer assignment years earlier in Vietnam, wherein I caused a couple of career changes in a few senior (to me) officers, told me that the sun was setting on my Marine Corps career. We began to discuss retirement from our beloved Marine Corps. It was a strained discussion, and initially, we both failed to reach any conclusion as to a particular course of action. I just wanted to prepare Lyn for me not being selected for promotion. For example, I simply knew, in my heart and mind, I would not be selected for lieutenant colonel.

Surprisingly, very surprisingly, in early 1981, I was selected for, attended, and completed the 124th Session of the FBI National Academy at Quantico, and attended the US Air Force Security Police Officer Advanced Course at the Lackland Air Force Base; both of these events occurred after attending the International Association of Chiefs of Police Conference in St Louis, MO in late 1980. I even took Lyn with me to St Louis, yet even with that done, I felt I was not going any higher in rank.

While attending the FBI National Academy, at the insistence of one of my classmates, I interviewed for a position with a sheriff's office. I thought nothing would come of it. But it caused Lyn and me to begin to make plans for life after the Marine Corps. Resumes were being dispatched to dozens of locations, with nary a one response, when out-of-the-blue; I'm offered a position with an Upstate New York Sheriff's Office; whereupon, I placed my request for retirement into motion. It seemed, at the time to be the only "straw" within my grasp.

To my total surprise, indeed complete shock, I was selected for promotion to lieutenant colonel, therefore it became tempting to stay, but the die had been cast. Lyn had heard about my selection for promotion from the Chief's wife while in the check-out line at the Commissary. The Marine Wives Grape Vine was alive and well. So, with a "bird" in hand and none in the bush, Lyn and I sat and talked. And, we made a decision. A joint decision.

To some, this may be a strange statement: One of the most rewarding events of my Marine Corps career occurred a few weeks before we hung up the green-suit and sailed an uncharted course into this thing called retirement. We were within days of vacating our quarters at Twenty-Nine-Palms, when a knock on my door at our quarters was answered to find our commanding general (Harold Glasgow I believe?) standing there. "Got a beer?" he asked.

We sat in lounge chairs in my back yard, enjoying a beer, looking out at the San Jacinto Mountains in the distance towering over Palm Springs down in the other end of the Morongo Valley, sipping our beer, and chatting. It was a typical June day in the high desert, about 120 degrees in the sun. Cool in the shade of our umbrella. It was an honor for me to have my commanding general, in this setting, ask me to reconsider my decision to retire. He was almost persuasive. I felt awed by the simplicity and directness of it all. He could have had me report to his office. He could have asked the chief of staff to talk to me. He could have simply ignored one Marine major who had placed the paperwork in motion to retire. Instead, it was one of those peaks. He chose to leave his office, come to my on base quarters, and sit in my back yard having a beer asking me to reconsider retirement.

As we finished our beers, we walked back through the quarters to the front door. After speaking with Lyn and expressing his regret at our decision, he stepped out our front door, stood for a second or two as his driver started his staff car, turned to me, and extended his hand. "Good luck, Ralph!" he said.

"Thank you, sir," was all I could think of to reply.

He turned to leave. Then, suddenly turned again and faced me. In that instant, I felt it was to relate to me something he had bottled up inside him and he needed to get it out now. "Ralph," he stated, looking directly into my eyes. "You did the right thing in Okinawa. What you did, and how you did it, is what caused you to be selected for lieutenant colonel. Think about it, major.

If you change your mind," he hesitated, "You know where to find me." He turned and walked to his staff car, and waved as his driver drove away.

That event on my front porch was my last peak as an active-duty Marine. It was a pretty high one. And, I for one, and Lyn for two did not consider it a strange statement.

A few weeks later my approval for retirement came in. I skipped the quarterly parade. We quietly departed our Corps of Marines while at the top of that peak, and slid into the ranks of Marine, (Retired).

What is obvious from the outcome of that event on my front porch at 29 Palms, is that everyone in the Marine Corps believed that it was me who had notified the Japanese National Police. Maybe they still do.

. . .

Entering the United States Marine Corps via the Reserves on 2 July 1955, and retiring from active duty to the retired list on 1 August 1981 gave me exactly twenty-six years of active service as a Marine. My Marine Wife had initially joined me as my girlfriend/fiancée in September 1958 and we married in December 1959. She was with me for twenty-three-and-a-half-years as I served on active duty as a Marine. Therefore, she is qualified to receive a commission as a Marine Wife, if there ever was, or is such a thing.

Although we retired from active duty, we did not leave the Marine Corps out of our lives. We have been active with Marine Corps activities and organizations right up to her death. She was an active participant in Marine Corps League matters in New York, Florida, and South Carolina, Mess Nights, Marine Corps Birthdays, other military oriented and themed organizations and events, such as Military Officers Association of America, and a self-created organization loosely referred to as "The Marine Corps Mess of Greenville (SC)," and also the Low Country Leathernecks, here locally. We never left the Corps. And, the Corps has never left us.

Looking back, it was with some reservation and a bit of hesitancy when I received that phone call, followed by a letter from the Sheriff in Monroe

County, New York offering me that job with a salary far above my active duty pay, and light-years from what I would make on Marine Corps retirement pay alone, after retiring. It came with a car, and family medical benefits also. Although I wouldn't mind being referred to as a "telephone colonel," (a Lieutenant Colonel who answers the telephone with the word "Colonel") we decided to retire. After 26 years, for me, and 23 years with my bride beside me, we would seek new horizons. I would become a "miracle-worker" (during my interview I told the sheriff he needed a miracle-worker for that job) for a few years. I accepted the offer to become the Superintendent of the Monroe County Jail system working for the Sheriff of Monroe County, New York.

While I still could have "found" my general (his parting words), we quickly traveled from California to look over the location of Rochester, New York, and the Monroe County Sheriff's Office and liked what we saw. Admittedly, the place had charm and the sheriff and his staff seemed to be accepting of a couple of outsiders from a military background and born southerners from the deep south state of Alabama. We loved Upstate New York. Making the move there, Lyn worked in several capacities. At Kodak, Bausch and Lomb, St John Fisher College, and Chase-Lincoln First Bank. At the bank she was secretary to Marshall "Marsh" Carter, a Marine officer, Vietnam War Veteran, and great boss. Other than in the Admissions Office at John Fisher, where she was lead-secretary, she was an excellent executive secretary in the other areas of endeavor.

I worked for four years with the Sheriff's Office, building, directing, creating and developing programs to make things better. I had and still have an admiration for the staff and even got along with the prisoners, especially the occasional organized crime figures incarcerated in our jail system. One particulate event with organized crime persons demands repeating: When we arrived at the Sheriff's Office we were briefed about organized crime and criminals. Look for darkened car windows, avoid certain restaurants, etc. Well, as Lyn would drive to St John Fischer College where she worked, a certain big, expensive car, with very dark windows would often pull beside her waiting for a light to change, or whatever. Lyn would squirm deeper into the car seat, avoiding anyone getting a good look at her, she believed! She thought perhaps real criminals, or possible criminals, were inside the car right next to her. Interestingly, she never mentioned it to me.

One particular day we (the sheriff's office organized crime division) had locked up several of these organized crime figures. It wasn't a big deal, but I always went through the jail and chatted with anyone locked up the night before. While on my rounds, I got to a holding cell and it was occupied by three of the guys I knew were into organized crime activities. Making normal inquiries and preparing to continue my rounds, I turned to depart the cell when one particular person said to me in strong Italian-English speech, "Superintendent, you say to that wife of yours, she ain't got no nothing to be afraid of. Ain't nobody gonna bother her. Tell her to quit scoot'in down behind her steering-wheel. She can't even see what's in front of her. It makes us laugh. She ain't got nuttin to be afraid of. You got my word." I told Lyn that story. She repeated it a hundred times. She had "protection" from the mob!

We were members of the Cooper-Marine American Legion Post, attended Marine Corps Birthday affairs, and I spoke at several Marine Corps events. Life was good with that sheriff's office; that is, until I had a falling-out with the Sheriff. When that occurred, the County Executive offered me the vacant position of Director of Emergency Preparedness. As such, I continued for two more years with Monroe County Government working closely with various industries locally, and the New York State Radiological Emergency Preparedness Group, as the Director of the Monroe County (NY) Office of Emergency Preparedness.

We bought some property, and had a cabin built overlooking Keuka Lake in the Finger Lakes Region which became our getaway, our sanctuary from the political hustle and bustle of the county and state. We did have a lot of friends in Upstate New York, would party a great deal, and started to travel overseas for vacations. We went to Spain, Morocco, Portugal, Aruba, and Cozumel, Mexico. The trip to Aruba was at the invitation of the Director of Security for Exxon, an old friend from Ft Gordon days and beyond, Claude Owen was director for security for EXXON Aruba. We even traveled to

Florida to attend a reunion of the 5th Warrant Officer Screening Course graduates. We attended numerous FBI National Academy Retraining Sessions in Toronto and Montreal, Canada and Hidden Valley Ranch in New York, near Lake George. We were a happy, contented couple.

Our children Deborah and Stoney Junior, both now high school graduates with some college, departed their parental nest while we lived in Upstate New York. Our son, Stoney had become more and more sullen and withdrawn since we had departed Okinawa. He dated a very nice girl in Rochester whose father owned a string of nursing homes. It never worked out. Eventually he followed his sister to another state.

Our daughter, Deborah departed to begin her new life elsewhere, after attending some college courses in New York, plus worked in some good jobs while in New York and in other locations. Finally, she found a very nice guy and they are still together.

Stoney Jr. married a very nice lady from Kentucky. She was a couple of years older, not that it counts for anything. Apparently, they had a difficult time. After his divorce from her and marriage (the second) to another person. We met her for the first time, once before they married and five or six times after they married. Frankly, they cut Lyn and me out of their lives. They had children. Our grandchildren. We only met two of them when they were still very small.

It seemed to be a situation wherein Lyn and I could gather with them with just us; however, when her parents were with the grandkids, we were often not included. A pattern of separation from us seeing or being with our grandkids developed. The last time was at Christmas, I think it was in 1998 (might have been much later), we took presents for our grandchildren only to discover the two children had been conditioned to actually be afraid of Lyn and me. It was painfully obvious we were, in their cultivated little minds, very bad people. When Lyn tried to kiss the younger one on the cheek, he blurted out a loud, "No! Don't you ever touch me! Don't touch me again!" while the parents, our son and daughter-in-law stood by smiling. Lyn said to me. "We're out of here!" We departed the scene. It was the last time we have seen any of them. Her parents were hostile to us at their wedding. None of the people Lyn had asked to be invited (her mother, daughter Deborah, and one of her sisters, Carol) to the wedding were ever invited. Very clearly Lyn and I had been written off their list of family members. We both have actually regretted attending their wedding.

For several years Lyn attempted to make contact. Once she got Stoney Jr. on the phone. When she asked if we could get together, Stoney replied, "Don't get your hopes up, mom. It's not going to happen."

Lyn dropped all attempts at contacting him. We, Lyn and I, discussed it at length several times, finally, it was Lyn who stated, "We, you and I, have a life to live. Let's not let anyone else tell us the terms of living it." Although, it did hurt, we simply wrote them off our Christmas Card List. We have had no contact at all with any of them since about Christmas in 1998, or whenever. It's been twenty-five years. Lyn and I have had, for the most part, except the times actually working for and within the workspace of Broward County Sheriff's Office, in Florida, a good life during those years in Florida and in South Carolina, until Lyn was diagnosed with cancer. We even tried to make the best of it during that time.

Lyn and I rounded out our venture with Monroe County, New York on a high note; however, the political scene was changing, getting more liberal as opposed to remaining conservative, which best suited our military oriented profile and lifestyle. I had several articles (opinions) printed in the newspaper in Rochester. I was on fairly good terms with most of the individuals in County Government. Our friends and co-workers even threw us a grand party prior to our departure. For some reason the Sheriff didn't attend.

I tired of the developing political gamesmanship, of on-again, off-again relations, and on a particularly cold-snowy February day, an old US Army friend from Fort Gordon days offered me a position with the Broward County Sheriff's Office in warm Fort Lauderdale, Florida. Without hesitation, I accepted. I didn't know it at the time but, Lyn and I were heading into the most difficult time in our lives while working within the Broward County Sheriff's Office, in Florida. It was something we had never experienced, and surely will never experience again. It was so unusual, so different from the "normal" which we had been accustomed to in all of our life's endeavors, I hesitate to write about it. It is still painful.

The following narrative is the personal opinion of me and of Lyn; however, I still retain copies of correspondence, letters, notes, journals, etc., to and from both Lyn and me with individuals within that Sheriff's Office which I can safely say, provides overwhelming evidence to support what I am about to proffer: To both of us, Lyn and me collectively, this was the most unethical, unfair, bunch of people we had ever been around, before or since. Both of us, especially me, spent most of our time and energy defending and somehow surviving a myriad of fabricated inuendoes, charges, and false accusations. That said, however, in all honesty, I must relate, here and now, there were some very professional, very dedicated, very honest individuals within this organization, but many were afraid and intimidated from speaking out in our behalf. Few became our friends. Very few!

Our problems stemmed from these few, well placed, exceptionally evil (my word) people constantly attempting to set me up on accusations of wrongdoing and have me fired. These individuals were high up the chain of command. Not THE Sheriff, in both sheriff's cases, but close enough to exercise their authority making both our lives very difficult and close to impossible. Indeed, at one juncture, I actually feared for my life.

The one who disappointed me the most was the, so-called "marine" (the small m again). The same one I assisted in getting into schooling at Fort Gordon, the one I invited to my home for a Marine Corps Birthday event, whose idea of Semper Fidelis was totally distorted. There were some additional people taking "jabs" at me, in both Administrations. Lyn and I consider them all to be equally despicable individuals.

This is what Lyn and I endured to survive and eventually retire (after ten years each) from the Broward County Sheriff's Office. I have always regretted departing from New York and relocating to Florida. It was a mistake, in one sense. Yet, in another, we outlasted the malevolent ones. We retired and have enjoyed our retirement benefits all these years. As you may surmise by now, it was Lyn who supported me and encouraged me when I was set-up and demoted twice, harassed repeatedly, and never received any accolade after establishing several programs in the jail and law enforcement systems of that Office. I was instrumental in installing an automated computer event reporting system within the law enforcement division, and a correctional boot-camp in the jail system, among other initiatives. I even had to "plea" in writing, to receive my earned merit increase in pay.

Lyn was devastated and cried each time I was demoted. I always will remember her crying, for me. It hurt her more than me. It only made me swear to endure, for her, and for our future. As a matter of fact, in order to be *allowed* to retire, I had to sign a document that I would never file a claim against the Sheriff's Office, or—here's the gist of the unspoken "suggestion"—I would not be allowed to retire. The purpose was quite clear, sign it and retire. Don't sign it and you don't retire. I signed it and never looked back. I have, had, and will not have any intention of filing any claim against these memorable people and having to actually see them again. To be in the vicinity of any of them would make me puke!

Here's just one example of how low-down these people were, they even faked a test result Lyn had taken while in the Training Division, where she had scored 90% on a written exam and they said she failed. Her answers were revised to be fabricated. I have documentation of that also. In the final analysis, we beat them. We endured their wrath and survived. But, the "scarlet letter" of the BSO will always be with us.

When I was asked, and accepted employment with that Office, things looked fine. I was a Commander of Operations with the Department of Detention. I had not been yet sworn in as a Sheriff's Deputy, so I applied for the law enforcement comparative-compliance course. Based on the State of Florida changing the required hours of class time, I had to attend and complete that course twice. Then, I completed the Corrections Officer comparative compliance course. Eventually, I was promoted to the rank of Major and was sworn in as a Deputy Sheriff, dual certified. I was hired into a sworn position, so actually I was never in a civilian role of a non-sworn position. Instead, I was always in a sworn position from day one.

Interestingly, around this time it was discovered I had colon cancer. Receiving an operation removing the tumor, and six months of chemo-therapy seemed to free me of cancer. During my recovery from cancer, is when my "marine" buddy was hired as my boss. That's when things began to go downhill for me. I was being attacked by cancer and him, at the same time.

My earlier immediate supervisor, the one who invited me to relocate to Florida, got himself into trouble and was fired. I was appointed as "acting" whatever he was. Essentially managing the entire Department of Detention's three confinement facilities, and special operations unit. I was not given a merit increase in salary. Anything I attempted to develop to make the operation better was either delayed or dismissed by my superiors.

Around the same time frame, the person who had asked Lyn to join the Sheriff's Office as his secretary, the Director of Internal Affairs, died of cancer. At his death, she was transferred out of the position she was initially hired for. She would be transferred again and again, apparently searching for the place or position that would be so difficult or distasteful for her, she would resign. Instead, she excelled and loved every position she was placed in, got along with the people she worked for and with, and excelled at just plain work ethic, working in Internal Affairs, Administration, Police District II, Training, Special Operations, the Stockade, etc. They would require some different means to undermine her sense of work ethics. They simply didn't know the sheer guts and fortitude of my Marine wife.

As mentioned, I was still recovering from cancer, still being treated when a new Detention Director was also hired who happened to be my "marine" buddy. Within days I was immediately given a "letter of caution" by him, and transferred to one of the three jail facilities, then demoted. From that point, the nightmare for Lyn and me started and never let up during that particular sheriff's Administration.

When a new sheriff was elected and assumed office, I was promoted to Lieutenant Colonel and was to be assigned as Detention (Jail) Director. Lyn was given a good position in Administration. All seemed well until another "new guy" was "found" for my job and I was reappointed as assistant "whatever."

Simply put, me and my bride started to lead interesting lives at the Broward County Sheriff's Office, again! Round two started and my life and that of my bride, again went downhill. Especially after the (newer) sheriff died in office, it became almost intolerable.

Somehow, we survived until eligible for retirement. Both of us put in highly professional, top-notch occupational work, and duties within our respective areas of responsibility. It's simply how we are made. After a long Marine Corps career, and a short stint in New York, combined with our life together, we had enough staying-power to go through that gauntlet, day-to-day, in order to survive, and get on with our lives. Mentally, I handled the constant "gotcha's" from my superiors; while it began to affect Lyn physically and mentally. It is unknown exactly why, or when, but she began to develop pain in different parts of her body, neck, back, shoulders, etc. Since working in that sheriff's office, it continued. Lyn has lived with constant pain. It's no wonder.

Several times, several individuals have asked me why did I stay (along with Lyn) with that bunch, in that job. The simple reason was, I had given up the New York position after six years because of the changing political climate and, my old friend offering me the position in Florida had painted a great picture. I hired on in March 1987, and didn't run into any hint of problems until July 1988 when my cancer was discovered. There's a part of me that believes the cancer was the end of my abilities to excel because I was written off as, a questionable health risk. Therefore, unacceptable for any vital position. The actual systemic harassing events didn't manifest until the "marine" was hired in about 1989 or 1990. So, I had the six New York years gone, and had three years of a ten-year retirement package already under my belt in Florida, so I didn't want to give up the three years, which along with the six, would have me disposing of nine years with nothing to show for it. Plus, add to that my thought process of sincerely believing that if we simply did our jobs and stayed the course working diligently and honestly for the Sheriff(s), nothing negative would happen to us. I was thinking Marine Corps [military] style ethics, where guys who didn't like you as a person would tell you to your face. I wasn't used to "back-shooters." Very wrong thinking on my part. I misjudged the concept of evil.

There was one other thing. I reasoned, as I began to understand evil and people who are users of evil means, that if they got rid of me, Lyn would not last long when they turned their wrath on her. My belief was, and still is, that she was being harassed to make me "crack." As long as I was there, I was the primary target. History has proven to me that I was correct. The first sheriff, after he was out of office, verified in a conversation with me over lunch together, that two particular people in his Administration wanted to get me fired. He named the two. And, told me he would not allow them to fire me. Admittedly, he did have a strange way of "protecting" me.

So, we move into a new Administration which we had assisted in getting elected, organizing and administrating, but it didn't take long. Higher-ups in the Administration tried and tried again to have me brought up on charges. When that failed again and again, a friend had told me, in confidence, that the new guy appointed over thought that me and Lyn, as apparent southerners from Alabama, were racially prejudiced. Today most everyone realizes that when you are painted with the racially-prejudice brush, it makes for an interesting future. They perfected that methodology.

Word was they were going to fire me, based on that particular conjured belief. If it was a belief and not just a ruse. I remember that particular day well, having been forewarned of the intent, but not the methodology. There was a meeting between the Human Resources Director, and my Director-Boss. During that meeting between the two of them, I was called into their mist. In the presence of the Human Resources person, the Director asked me pointedly, "Are you an Indian?"

My response was, "Yes!" At that point I was summarily dismissed.

As I exited the office and was closing the door, I overheard the Human Resources Director tell my boss, "See. I told you he was. So, you can't . . ." I didn't hear the rest. Apparently, the concept or plan of firing me was placed on hold. But the *treatment* continued.

I can't recall all, there were so many over the span of two Administrations. Once my issued marked Sheriff's Patrol car was struck while parked in a legally assigned parking spot in the Sheriff's Office parking lot by an unknown other vehicle. I was charged with having an accident. Apparently, I caused the other unknown car to strike mine. Very unusual process. Oh, when I asked for a hearing, the charges were dropped. It gets better. I had to take a polygraph test about whether or not I told my boss about one of my deputies having unauthorized relations with an inmate. I was on authorized vacation when this event happened. I was convinced I had mentioned it to him, while he said I didn't. After the story of me not telling him was told to me several times that I failed to notify the Director of the event, although it was public knowledge, I alone, was required to take a polygraph. The polygraph operator from Internal Affairs, the office which had been attempting to get me with something, anything, said I was "deceptive." Now, Sheriff's Policy and Procedure Manual dictated that the accuser must also take a "poly." It never happened. I was charged and demoted from Major to Captain.

I was demoted again under the new Administration. Lyn and I assisted the new Sheriff during his campaign. He won. I was given the rank of Lieutenant Colonel and placed in charge of the Jail and Corrections Bureau. Then, a new guy is discovered somewhere, some said, on an airplane, and is appointed as Director. A friend in that particular Administration told me I was not of the particular race (they assumed me to be White or Caucasian, yet I was recorded as Native American in sheriff's administration documents) the Sheriff wanted as Jail Director. When, under the newer sheriff, after a few weeks with this new guy, I start to hear that my wife and I are racially prejudice. I hear it from numerous sources. Eventually, when all the several attempts to charge me or accuse me of something failed, and the plan to fire me based on the assumption I was prejudice against some race of people failed to work out for them, I was simply summarily and quietly demoted from Lieutenant Colonel to Deputy Sheriff. No discussion, no charges, no nothing. One day I'm a Lieutenant Colonel, the next day, I'm a Deputy Sheriff. Big loss of pay.

As a Deputy Sheriff, I finished my career with the Broward County Sheriff's Office working for one of the few honest professional department heads, Jim Buani, in the Information Services Bureau. He protected me and ran interference for me to get the required time in to retire. Without his assistance,

I perhaps would never have made it. Matter of fact, I understand he was fired for refusing to fire me. You can't make this stuff up.

Lyn and I were simply lucky to each have survived ten years with that Sheriff's Office. I retired in March 1997, as a Deputy Sheriff and Lyn retired in September 1997. The sheriff's office personnel director initially attempted to have me retire as a civilian, which would be cutting retirement pay and delaying my ability to immediately draw it. They tried; however, the State of Florida and The Florida Retirement System overrode their intent and rightly retired me as a high-risk (sworn Sheriff's Deputy).

In each of our cases, we had to "eat up" our unused vacation and sick time so we would not receive any additional pay for it. Why? We'll never really know. Just part of the harassment package. All I can say is somebody(s), wanted to ensure I was constantly on-guard for dismissal or demotion and the harassment of Lyn was designed to have me break-down and retaliate or do something equally stupid. Most of the harassment came from my "marine buddy," and two others equally positioned "inciters of mayhem." Interestingly, the two in the first Administration were, like me—graduates of the FBI National Academy at Quantico, Virginia

Lyn always believed it was because those closest to the sheriff's (yes, we lived through two of them) knew of and had surveyed my background and previous assignments and accomplishments and wanted to ensure I was never considered for advancement. Especially advancement over them. I was a threat. Turf protection? Racism? Jealousy? Combination thereof? Whatever! Take your pick. All I can say is this missive only describes some of what happened to Lyn and me. I still have no idea why. But I have a treasure-trove of documentation.

Before departing Broward County and the Broward Sheriff's Office, let me say, that Lyn and I, in spite of our *treatment* within that sheriff's office, slipped into some very enjoyable and enchanting times together while in Florida. We would take voyages on the MV *Discovery* from Port Everglades to and from the Bahamas. As sheriff's employees, it was cheap. Real cheap. For about $19.00 each, we could board, have breakfast, sail to the Bahamas, before docking, have lunch, disembark, shop, gamble, have a couple of drinks, reboard, sail for home, have dinner, and enjoy the lounge before docking at Port Everglades and driving home. We also took our first-ever week-long cruise on a cruise ship. We had a friend in the 911 Center who was also a part-time travel agent. She took care of us.

Our first cruise was into and out of the Panama Canal. It was enjoyable so we did more cruising. Most of them in the Caribbean and once or twice on the western side of Mexico. Our longest was from Acapulco, Mexico to Fort Lauderdale via the Panama Canal for ten days. Before we each retired, we went to Europe on a fly-rail vacation. Flew from Ft Lauderdale to Paris, on the rail to Brussels, and, again on the rail to Amsterdam, then flying to London, and on the rail back to Paris via the Chunnel. Finally, flying back home. It was a great vacation, taken right as I was retiring and Lyn had another few months to go.

While in Broward County we lived in Plantation, Florida in a nice home with a pool and partially covered patio. We had a boat we had purchased which we kept in a marina in Plantation Key in Monroe County, Florida. These were our *escape* places. These were the places we reenergized our lifetime batteries. We had almost no friends from the Sheriff's Office. We were too "hot" to associate with! I guess our only quasi-friend was a person I hired when I was acting as director of detention, Charles Barnes, a good guy with a nice wife.

. . .

So, from Broward County Florida, after we retired, we moved to Punta Gorda, Florida. But not before I hired on with the Monroe County, Florida Sheriff's Office in the Florida Keys. Lyn was still working for BSO. I hired on because I was offered a great job, and I wanted to see if Broward County had "blacklisted" me. In the process for hiring, I passed the polygraph for entry into the Sheriff's Office as a sworn deputy, with the same set of questions asked by Broward when I was demoted for "lying" to my "marine" boss. I had disclosed all my trials and tribulations with BSO to the Personnel staff in Monroe County during my hiring process. I was totally honest. They covered the same questions and I gave the same answers. Then, I was hired.

This was the deal I was offered with Monroe County, Florida Sheriff's Office, I was told I'd be assigned to the Ocean Reef Community on the north end of Key Largo. Field Training (familiarization training) was to be conducted on the job with another deputy at that same location who happened to be a field training officer (FTO). I was to work solely at this exclusive community as long as I was with Monroe County. When that offer suddenly came with caveats, modifying the initial agreement, I retired, again.

The caveat which was thrown in a few months later, was I was to drive every work day from my home, which was now in Sunrise, Florida, to Key West, a distance of about 165 miles, for Field Training and work in other districts to become "familiar" with all of Monroe County. I was with them about two or three months. My guess was and still is that Broward talked to Monroe, and the situation changed for me. I say that now because, later, when Lyn and I moved to Greenville County, in South Carolina, I volunteered to work as a non-paid volunteer with Greenville County Sheriff's Office. Even the Greenville County sheriff at the time, seemed excited and positive with that idea. I filled out a proper application and Greenville Sheriff's Office was to call Broward County Sheriff's Office in Florida. We never heard a word from Greenville County Sheriff's Office after they contacted the Broward County Sheriff's Office.

Nonetheless, we moved to Charlotte County on the west-coast of Florida, and moved into a house we had built in Burnt Store Marina, in Punta Gorda. We were both now retired-retired, and breathed a long sigh of relief having survived the most distasteful indigestible organization we have ever had the displeasure of associating with. And, the most intractable, incorrigible individuals who has ever walked the earth. With a few, very few exceptions.

Moving from Broward County Florida was like relocating from Hell to Heaven, when we arrived in Charlotte County on the Gulf of Mexico side of Florida. Moving in to our new home at Burnt Store Marina, we attended The Retired Officers Association (TROA),now called Military Officers Association of America (MOAA) dinner meeting where we made a few friends, eventually, from that start, we joined a Yacht Club, then a Boat Club, and finally a Country

Club, garnering in the process a great group of friends and we did much travelling and socializing together.

We had annual theme parties, ours was a St Patrick's Day bash each year. Others picked up any of the holiday themes and designed a party around it. We (Lyn and I) hosted a St. Patrick's Day party every year for ten years with over fifty people in attendance at each event. Even had real peat-fires outside and bangers and mash on the menu and live Irish music. Lyn joined the Charlotte County Symphony League. She painted and sold her work. We were happy, even later moving a mile or so down the road to a larger house in Burnt Store Lakes, continuing to travel, party, do art work and generally do what retired folks do. We enjoyed life. Lyn was the "hit" of almost all our social engagements on the west coast of Florida. She had her shopping groups, her breakfast, and dinner groups and our party groups.

Lyn, in Punta Gorda, Florida

We had not been living in Punta Gorda long when I decided to attend a Travel School. The kind that produces travel agents. It was *The Travel School of Sarasota* (FL). It was enjoyable and after graduation I got a part-time job as a travel agent with an agency in Port Charlotte, Florida. Selling travel was fun and the agency also sold insurance. Lyn obtained a job as a secretary with the insurance side of the business. Having been a travel agent for only a month or two, and receiving a call from the owner of the Travel School of Sarasota asking me to manage and teach at his new agency (travel school) in Fort Myers, Florida, I accepted the offer.

I began to manage and teach travel at the Fort Myers location. It too was much fun. Lyn worked in the insurance business for a few months until she assumed more responsibilities with the Charlotte County Symphony League. Then, her art work kicked in resulting in more time at her art work. We were on a roll. Then everything came to a halt after 9/11!

I have failed to mention our continued travel with friends. We travelled to Ireland a few times staying in Farms, Pubs and Bed and Breakfast places. We even took a three-day trip to stay in an original 1930s Sears and Roebuck catalog ordered and assembled house which was now a B&B in a town just north of Tampa. Eight of us spent the night there. Several of our cruises were out of Port Manatee on an old cruise ship, often to nowhere. We cruised the southern Caribbean, sailed to the Bahamas, and even really sailed on a barefoot cruise on an actual sail-boat, SV *Mandalay* with Windjammer Cruises, from the island of Grenada on 1 or 2 September 2001, arriving in Caracas, Venezuela via Puerto La Cruz, on 10 September 2001 and going through the tightest of security before boarding an American Airlines flight to Miami. Arriving in Miami about 2000 (8pm) on 10 September, the next day, 9/11 greeted us. America and the world changed forever.

SV Mandalay of Windjammer Cruises-Lyn aboard SV Mandalay 1 Sep-10 Sep 01

I taught my last class after 9/11 happened. The travel business grinded almost to a halt, so, I found part-time work with Thrifty Auto Rental for a few months as a night manager. From there, I hired on part-time with *The Sun Sentinel* Newspaper. It was a "gofer" job. I sold subscriptions, conducted surveys, proof-read, whatever was needed. Lyn was still deep into art and symphony business.

We sold our boat, but still boated. Many of our friends had boats. Some of them big-big boats. We did "raft-ups," Christmas boat parades, and, the most interesting event of all. On New Year's Eve, 1999, as the millennium descended upon us and we waited for aircraft to fall from the sky and ships to run aground, our group of twenty or so somebodies, decided to bring in the New Year in a most unusual manner. The men dressed in black tuxedo jacket, white shirt and black tie over white Bermuda-shorts and tennis shoes and the women dressed in in long or short cocktail attire and tennis shoes to bring in the year 2000 aboard an 87-foot yacht by the name of *Freedom*, docked on an island off the coast of west Florida which the CIA used to train the Cuban

Brigade destined to invade and liberate Cuba from Castro. That didn't go too well in Cuba, but we had a hell of a great party, aboard *Freedom*, afterward each couple crawled into our assigned sleeping berths, and woke up around daybreak in the year 2000. Airplanes still were in the air and boats were still on the water. Clocks still worked revealing the correct time and the earth still turned toward the east. Stoney and Lyn Bates were still in love. All was well.

With the exception of the Broward County Sheriff's Office, we did enjoy our Florida sojourn. Our last fly-cruise vacation with our Florida friends was to Rome for three days, then to the port of embarkation and we sailed all along the coast of Italy, Croatia, Sicily, France and Spain. Great vacation lasting two weeks. Very memorable! Now we had been in Florida for twenty-one years. Ten with those at that "sheriff's" office and ten in Punta Gorda on the west coast, as retired-retired. Based on our lifestyle and records of frequent movements, it was time for the Bates couple with vagabond blood flowing through our veins and arteries, to go elsewhere.

. . .

Our daughter, Deborah and Vince lived in a great location and invited us to come up and look the place over. We did pay her a visit, in a most unusual way. We went camping. Had to purchase all the camping gear as we hadn't been camping since our California days at Camp Pendleton in the 1960s. Camping for several days on Lake Hartwell on the South Carolina side, we visited nearby Greenville, fell in love with the atmosphere and location and decided to relocate to Greenville. The ingrained military style of constant relocations had become an irresistible lifestyle urge.

We met a very nice gentlemen who, at the time, was involved with the Greenville Symphony Orchestra and was instrumental in assisting us in adapting to Greenville living and meeting new friends. While getting settled, one thing led to another and we found ourselves in with another group of friends. The main difference in our Greenville friends from our Florida friends was that our new group in Greenville had, for the most part, already been formed and we joined them; whereas, most of our Florida friends entered our arena, or circle of friends, patchwork-fashion over time.

Whether or not it was planned, we seemed to follow a pattern copied from our last ten years in Florida. Lyn joined the Greenville Symphony League. It was similar to the one in Charlotte County, Florida. We purchased a home in Taylors, SC, moved in and again, we traveled a bit, joined a private club, partied, and began to enjoy life, even to the point of organizing a loose informal Marine Corps Birthday group which we called "The Marine Corps Mess of Greenville." We began with twenty-six attendees celebrating the Corps Birthday, and, when we departed Greenville, for the American Territory of Guam, we had over a hundred attendees celebrating Marine Corps Birthday in style. Lyn was highly instrumental in planning, coordinating and setting-up each Marine Corps Birthday celebration.

Top: Lyn at head table Marine Corps Mess of Greenville Marine Corps Birthday Celebration. Bottom: Lyn assisting the general with cake cutting at same celebration

One thing that we had very much in common with our friends in Greenville was that we enjoyed travel. We sailed from Charleston to the Bahamas, and to Bermuda at another time. We also cruised the Caribbean several times. Lyn and I enjoyed a fabulous air, land, cruise vacation around South America, just the two of us. We flew from Greenville, via Miami to Buenos Aires, Brazil where we lingered four days, then boarded a cruise ship for a voyage around the southern tip of South America to Valparaiso, Chile, staying for four days in Santiago, Chile before flying back to Greenville via Miami. Our ship stopped in numerous locations In Brazil, Uruguay, Argentina and Chile during the Voyage. It was fabulous and expensive! But we deserved it.

Both of us began attending classes at Furman University's Osher Lifelong Learning Institute (OLLI) where I began to teach some classes along with attending classes at the same time. From one of those classes regarding writing which I attended came our first book, an anthology containing fifty-two true stories from thirty-seven different authors. Its title is *Short Rations For Marines*. That began a labor of love for Lyn and me. She purchased the *Chicago Manual of Style*, searched the internet to copy, paste, and print her own manual of writing style, and became my most ardent critic, proofer, editor, researcher, and writing assistant *par excellence*!

Since that first publication there have been others, a few published historical novels, books, short stories and articles (for newspapers and magazines), while others were simply preparing someone else's manuscript for publication, finishing an unfinished manuscript from someone who had died before completing their work, in short, helping others prepare or complete manuscripts. Although my name is adorning much of our work as author; my Lyn was always the guiding light, the researcher, the unadorned, unrecognized force of momentum in developing and completing each piece of literary work. She was the other half of me.

As we were finishing up the first anthology, I was teaching a class at OLLI on amphibious warfare. Several of my students asked where we could visit to see and learn more about the subject. Lyn suggested I take them to the National Museum of the Marine Corps outside Quantico Marine base in Virginia.

Several members of my class and I took the trip. It was highly educational. While there, I took them to dinner at The Globe and Laurel Restaurant, owned by an old Marine Corps friend Major Rick Spooner, USMC (Ret). While there I met Patrick Timothy Brent (PT Brent) a Marine in his own right and an entrepreneur of sorts, who got me interested in writing my first historical-novel about John Archer Lejeune. Although we hired an editor, that project propelled Lyn deeply and permanently into the role of my editor-in-chief, researcher, proof-reader and idea developer. In all my writings, she played a vital role. I sincerely believe she is guiding me as this book is being written.

Although writing became the forefront forte of our time in Greenville, we also just happened to attend (as I was the invited guest-speaker) a Marine Corps Birthday celebration twice in Lisbon, Portugal and once in Brussels, Belgium at the invitation of the Marine Security Guard Detachments at each of these United States Embassies. It was an honor to be so invited and attending those functions. In other areas, we participated in obtaining season tickets at the Symphony and Off-Broadway shows in downtown Greenville at the Peace Center. Then too, we enjoyed eating-out in addition to weekly dinners at our club. We got along with each other; however, this was a different group from our Florida friends. A very different group.

Lyn continued to have medical issues, treated mostly by injections and ablations to neck and spine. Her onion allergy became more acute and, as time passed, unfortunately, or perhaps fortunately in the long run, her "friends" slowly and methodically began to distance themselves from her. I hadn't noticed, but I did notice she was quieter, more withdrawn, and Lyn was anything but withdrawn. Finally, one day while we were at home, she began to cry. I get upset when someone makes my Lyn cry. I hugged her and asked, "What's wrong, Sweetheart?"

Still crying, she responded, "Haven't you noticed that none of the women talk to me anymore?" I admitted I hadn't.

So, the next time we were with several of our friends having dinner at the club, I paid very close attention. When we joined our table of eight, and as the evening progressed, very clearly none of the women said a word to Lyn. She was right, she was being ostracized for some unknown reason. It's not my usual behavior, but I began to seethe, and eventually, at a boiling point, made a scene. Exercising little restraint, in my righteous indignation, I verbally blasted those at my table that evening, took my bride by the hand and proceeded to exit the club. I was loud, and several days later went to the club manager and apologized to him and the staff. He was gracious enough to accept my explanation and apology

Lyn explained to me that her friends had excluded her from their monthly breakfast meetings, which she had initiated. I had a similar monthly breakfast with our male friends. We did that in Florida, so Lyn initiated a monthly breakfast meeting with the ladies. As we discussed the situation in some length and detail, it seems her constant verbal jousting with various wait-staff about her onion allergy apparently embarrassed or disturbed some of those she dined with. How was it affecting Lyn?

She was always having to explain her allergy in detail, only to be frequently further embarrassed, for example, when she would be served a hamburger with an onion ring on top of the bun, after she has emphasized her allergy, or when she would have a salad with onion in the mixture and send it back, sometimes with the kitchen staff simply removing the onion and re-severing the items with the juice still on the ingredients. To some, perhaps it might be considered "making a scene." On a few occasions, she fell very ill at the scene while eating out.

This allergy affected her greatly, physically and more so mentally as time went by. This is why Lyn has many times said, "If I could be granted only one wish, it would be to rid myself of this onion allergy. It (the onion allergy) has caused me more bad episodes than anyone would ever believe." She has said those words, or similar phraseology, again and again through the last few years.

• • •

The two of us, with some assistance early on with paid professional editors, completed and published the two books *Short Rations For Marines*, an anthology, and *A Marine Called Gabe*, a historical-novel of the life and legend of John

Archer Lejeune (pronounced luh-jern). And, almost at the same time-frame, we were completing a manuscript written by a Marine who had died before he could finish it. The manuscript had been safeguarded for many years by his step-daughter. She tasked us to complete it and to prepare it for publishing as titled, *Back Step*, a fictional novel, under the authors name Burnard Winburn, a Marine Master-Gunnery Sergeant, (Ret), deceased.

While finishing and assisting the step-daughter in publishing *Back Step*, we were also planning a fact-finding trip to Guam. An old friend, a fellow Marine, Adolf Sgambelluri, a Chamorro of Guam had written a short story published in my Anthology titled *Short Rations For Marines*. It was an enticing story of a Chamorro double-agent during World War II on Guam, and being a writer, and author of several books and magazine articles, and having an inquisitive and supportive Marine wife, we wanted to investigate the feasibility of writing a book of "Sgamby's" dad during World War II. That was the initial purpose of our planning a trip to Guam. We wanted a fact-finding-mission to determine if we were thinking logically. Was there sufficient information about our friend's dad, Adolfo Camacho Sgambelluri, or "Sgambe," as he was called, to write a book?

After the "incident" at our club and the reaction from a surprising number of our former friends, we stopped use of the club scene. We also reached a decision that going to Guam with the almost certainty of finding sufficient information to consider a book writing project again, that we might be required to spend a lengthy stay on the Island. Taking the "bull by the horns," my Marine Wife, Lyn and I purchased a round trip flight to Guam to meet up with my old friend Sgamby (with a y, the dad was with an e), and do some on-site research regarding World War II, the Marines, Naval Governors of Guam, the Chamorro, the American government, and the Japanese of that era.

Lyn's feelings of being somewhat devastated, gradually turned to anger, that she had associated with some people who would be so unfeeling toward a "friend" with a problem or condition beyond their ability to control. Was it just her allergy to the onion that caused all this? Was it other medical maladies? We'll never know. We actually don't care. Lyn would say: "Friends just don't do that to friends," even if they were allergic to the air we breathe or the sunshine that warms our bodies, friends don't do that. It began with jokes about onions, then snide remarks, onward to clandestine contempt, followed by old-fashioned silent treatment and finally after given the silent treatment—community "banishment."

After my outburst at the club, fully half of our, so-called friends actually asked the club management to dismiss or discharge us from the club. When that didn't work out to their satisfaction, we were informed, by a "group" spokesperson that we were disallowed to sit at a table with any and all members of that particular group, our former "friends." Lyn made a statement, if I can remember it properly, went something like this: "The *royalty* had ejected the *peasants* from their mist." Only one couple within our group, a Marine and his wife, told us they would dine with us anytime, anywhere. But clearly, it was time to seek other adventures, in another venue.

So, we went to Guam for a month of fact-finding, and when we returned from Guam after doing enough research to conclude we should write a book. There was more than enough material to do more research and start writing the book. Not about Sgambe, per se, but about the Chamorro, the indigenous population of Guam, before, during and after World War II. The book became: *An American Shame: The Abandonment of an Entire American Population*. It would become our boldest, most expensive, and most ambitious project we had ever undertaken. So, for the first time we seriously considered departing the Greenville area and relocating, permanently! Perhaps even on Guam. However, after actually "living" on Guam, researching and writing, we narrowly ruled out moving permanently to Guam, then the dilemma became where to go. It was then we began to talk of all the places we have lived, beginning with Parris Island, South Carolina in the Lowcountry, where we started our married life together, and the more we talked, the more we mentioned the words "Low-Country."

. . .

Though we have traveled to many locations, Guam was the most fruitful in capturing the lives of many loyal Americans which most Americans have never heard of. Most Americans haven't a clue of the Chamorro of Guam, especially during World War II in the Pacific. We told their story accurately, honestly, and as tactfully as allowed with the passage of time; however, the Department of the Interior and military and naval Exchanges on Guam and in mainland America, apparently don't wish to have it told, or sold through their mediums. It's another *American Shame*.

We had spent a month in Guam doing research, driving around the Island, talking with anyone who would talk to us, spending time with Sgamby and Rose, his wife, the President of the University of Guam, and we secluded within the walls of the Micronesia Area Research Center (MARC) at the University of Guam. Very clearly, there was more than sufficient material for a book, but not about Sgamby's dad, Sgambe, although he would become a part, a very important part of the story. It was of the American people of Guam who were literally abandoned by the United States government to the Japanese Imperial invaders and occupied by Imperial Japan for 31 months of torture, brutality, rape, and ultimate survival as a society of captives. We had returned home, shared the excitement with what was left of our "friends," firmed up plans, and began to execute them.

. . .

We sold our home in Taylors, South Carolina, put all our worldly possessions into storage, packed two suitcases, a camera and laptop, and departed for Guam for an undetermined length of time. It ended up to be a total stay of about eight months to complete research for the book. It became a labor of love for the two of us. We met and associated with people from all walks of life on Guam. We met active-duty military personnel, retired military living on Guam, former and current government officials, and average citizens while we stayed in a hotel room, drove a rental car, and visited almost every part of the island. Gradually, we became accepted. Chamorros, by their nature and by the fact they have not always been dealt with fairly by the US government and, from time-to-time by several of us "mainlanders," as they call us, it was difficult to be trusted at first, but day-by-day, we began to earn the trust and loyalty so necessary to be accepted.

Lyn would say that she actually became a blond, blue-eyed Chamorro before we returned to the low-country of South Carolina, purchase a home in Mt. Pleasant, SC, moved in, finished and published the book, and returned to Guam to release it to the public. It is, at this time, the most desirable time to write in this particular publication of the fabulous, awesome, magnificent adventures the two of us encountered actually living on Guam and interacting with history on a daily basis; however, that impulse must be resisted. The book *An American Shame* explains it all. Please read the book!

That, 'returned to Guam,' was, in a word or two, extraordinarily amazing! Quite an adventure. It was our first and only time we actually felt like celebrities. Maybe we were! Unfortunately, apparently because of some of the truthful, researched and documented content in the texts (we pulled no punches), and a, shall we say, initially a controversial image on the front cover. To some mainlanders then living or working on Guam, simply thought it (the cover) was inappropriate. The military exchanges, who had agreed previously for book-signings, refused to allow them. Even the Department of the Interior disallowed the book to be sold in the bookstore of the *War in the Pacific Museum* on Guam; however, the reception we received from the mostly Chamorro population of Guam, the Government of Guam, and from the University of Guam, totally advocated for our book and publicized it constantly.

On day one, after arriving on Guam to release the book for sale, we were on an early morning popular radio talk-show, then in the evening we conducted a book signing at the University of Guam, filling a large room with political and ideological opposites, all vying for signed copies. This was followed by a couple of appearances on television, newspaper interviews, and invitations galore to feast after feast, group meetings after group meetings, church festivals after church festivals. We met with all the mayors of the villages, and the governor met us on two occasions and penned a *The Governor's Award*, document presented to us by the governor himself. Two previous governors, a Democrat and a Republican advocated for us and assisted us in obtaining vital interviews. Sgamby was most helpful in opening doors marked closed. The people of Guam, especially the Chamorro population purchased hundreds of copies, showered us with affection, and invited us to event after event while we were on that island. Bookstores on Guam carried our book. Even after returning to the mainland (the United States proper), from here in the low country, we were invited by the Governor of Guam to join the Pacific Islands Group in attending the Presidential Inauguration festivities in Washington DC for the elected President Donald Trump. Here, in the low country we have moved from one Guam Liberation Day celebration event to another and another for the next several years selling the popular book until stopped by COVID-19.

Guam was a dream come true in mini-format. Returning home via Hawaii we were assisted and entertained by old Marine Corps friends living on Oahu, the Bates, John and Stephanie of Hawaii (no relation), and PT Brent among them. Hawaii has been our stopover location many, many times as we have crisscrossed the vast Pacific Ocean. Indeed, my bride and I have traveled the world-together!

. . .

Parris Island is where Marines are made. For us, it is also where my Marine wife was made. Her acceptance into a Marine Corps (military) lifestyle as the wife of an E-4 Acting Sergeant who happened to be a Marine Drill Instructor, is, by itself, an amazing transformation. Her accomplishments over trials, and difficulties starting out as the wife of a low-ranked Marine, even walking to the Exchange and Commissary to purchase needed items while our car was "in-hock" in the impound lot, speaks volumes of the determination to do what is necessary, not necessarily what you want to do. Rather than cry, or complain, as many do, she sucked it up, adapted and persevered. Not bad for an eighteen-year-old, never been left alone before, new bride. She was exposed, nurtured and matured as a Marine Wife in coastal South Carolina, and would take that foundation with her to grow and ultimately excel in honoring the title Marine Wife, all her life. We would eventually go back to our roots, the Low Country of South Carolina. It is where we would reside until the day she died.

Today, as I write this, in remembrance of my lifetime companion Lyn, even in my grief, I continued to enjoy the Carolina Lowcountry. We had, and I continue to have friends, especially at St Andrews Church in Mt. Pleasant where I feel most comfortable. A friend, Paul Watters, who lost his wife Pat a few weeks before I lost my Lyn, was instrumental in involving me in several support groups. I am most grateful. I'm also grateful to Paul Watters, and to Lindsey Christmas, who is also a writer; and, both of them are volunteers at the Maritime and Naval Museum, for taking the time to review and offer pro-posed amendments to, and suggestions for this publication.

Lyn enjoyed various groups, especially the East Cooper Republican Women's group, I volunteered at the Patriots Point Maritime and Naval Mu-seum, joined the I'm Not Dead Yet (INDY) lunch meeting group through the website *Meet Up*, the 88 Club Breakfast meeting group, joined Low Country Leathernecks, and both of us attended each Marine Corps Birthday celebration these last few years until Lyn simply became too ill to attend. Even during her weakness from the cancer and chemicals used to diminish it, she would occa-sionally insist on getting a shower, dressing with assistance, applying her make-up, arranging her hair, and attending Marine Corps oriented functions with the Low Country Leathernecks. It was just the Semper Fi in her.

While we have lived in the Low Country of South Carolina, we have trav-elled. In addition to the sojourns to Guam, we have visited Portugal for the fourth or fifth time, once meeting friends from Guam there. My bride and I visited the Canary Islands of Spain. We had wanted to make that visit for over forty years. Finally, we did it. Also, we visited our Florida time-share, and vis-ited our old friends on the West Coast of South Florida, who have remained there in Florida from our days of living there, while shunning Broward County totally. Lyn continued to assist delving into research, correct my writings for *Leatherneck* and *Marine Corps Gazette* magazine articles plus the occasional local newspaper opinions page, and one additional book which we completed and published about Patriots Point Volunteers titled *Short Rations from Patriots Point Volunteers*. Sadly, that book is not sold at the gift shop at Patriots Point Naval Museum gift/book shop.

Her favorite place was in the evening hours, with a glass of wine and a book, she would sit in our sun-room facing west, looking out at the pond, trees, flowers, birds, and butterflies behind our house. My bride had always been a lover of nature. Watching butterflies dart from blossom to blossom, enjoying squirrels climbing and jumping from tree to tree. Often, she'd comment on such things as the wind whispering through pine trees, evening shadows walking through our property as sun-set quickly approached, and other observations of simple things of nature that captivated her. Enjoying travelling country to country. Just enjoying life. Then, cancer struck. Even through her last few weeks and months, she preferred sitting, with that glass of wine and a book, at her favorite spot, out in our sunroom, watching the sun slowly fade into evening and on into darkness, she was just enjoying every moment, every second of life.

Lyn, Feb 2022, her 80th birthday, in her sunroom,
a glass of wine, a book, an orchid, enjoying life.

. . .

There are no words that could be uttered by any human to convey the intense admiration in my heart and soul for my departed bride who has accompanied me for over sixty-four years, and being just shy of sixty-three years of marriage. She was one tough, caring, exceptional woman, using every ounce of her being to live, to fight against the invasion of this mutant of cancer, experiencing elation for her progress and dismay at the eventual advance of the mutant cells. She wanted to live desperately. We had plans, together, for our future. But she was also aware that our future was to be much shorter than we had hoped for. We still had dreams and songs to sing, but her energy was diminishing. Her last days were a display of resolute dignity in an undignified chain of human events involving the process of slowly dying. Several weeks earlier, she had made a difficult and logical decision to cease the chemo-therapy which seemed to be more debilitating than the cancer. It was sapping her strength. She became incapable of caring for herself and enjoying life for what it is supposed to be. But anyone observing her would never realize it. She spoke, and dreamed, and acted optimistically, well-knowing of the end which would be her companion for the remainder of the journey. She was remarkable!

She would enter Palliative Care followed by Hospice Care while remaining at home in her familiar and comforting surroundings. We reminisced frequently about our life together. She would sometimes wear my old Marine Corps T-shirts, and even my old utility cover (cap) to keep the sun out of her eyes sitting in the sunroom. On many of these days we would verbally and emotionally drift back to our life's finest hours, the Corps, our Corps. It was her Corps just as much, if not more so, than mine. Ours was a life well-lived, on the peaks and even in the valleys. Her spirit never faded.

She lit and carried the lamp of life, holding it high, guiding the two of us on our pathway through this thing called a lifetime. Lifetimes always presents many twists and turns, even a few detours which tended to reroute us as we move along. She would find our way back. I could not have found my way without her. We began with just the two of us and ended as it began with just the two of us. We were alone together. I had kissed her as she lay in her hospice provided bed in our living room covered with a sheet and her grey National Museum of the Marine Corps blanket, she had purchased on one of our many book-signing trips to Quantico and the National Museum of the Marine Corps Gift Shop/Bookstore. She could observe her favorite view through the sun-room window from there. I kissed her. She smiled, I turned, moved some things out of my chair to sit beside her, glancing across toward her she was seemingly resting peacefully, appearing to be asleep. Her eyes were closed and she was very still, not breathing. She had passed away. My life's companion was gone.

. . .

This is the end of a simple, truthful, unvarnished account relating some small portions of the life of my bride Linda "Lyn" Gale Bates; interestingly, she would not have appreciated, nor allowed any other method of story-telling, as she wanted no gathering, no viewing, no casket, no eulogy to be spoken such as at a traditional funeral, only to be cremated, and brought home, where she again resides. She wanted no gathering and had said to me, if no one wanted to visit her while she was alive, she didn't want them visiting her dead. I told her that her wishes would come to pass; however, I would write about her. "Lyn, I do intend to write about you. I might even make it a book," I had said a few weeks before she died.

She gave me that impish smile saying, "How are you going to do that with-out me?"

My response was, "I'll simply try!" This has been my try!

. . .

She was right. She had asked, "How are you going to do that without me?" It hasn't been easy without her. I'm just a simple writer not a very gifted one, never well known, but for this—I must try! I'm simply one Marine, of many thousands of Marines, active, honorably discharged, or those now retired that have had that wonderful companion by their side. I'm nowhere near being what is generally referred to as a great Marine, with nary a single heroic feat of achievement. That profile and title was never my fit. Just a Marine who performed any duty assigned or assumed as best I could, lived a life as best as one can, sometimes on the top of the peaks and, sometimes in those deep depressive valleys; but with Lyn by my side, always gaining momentum to rise up from that depression which sometimes lay siege to our progress. On the top, the bottom, or in between, I've always been accompanied by the greatest companion anyone, Marine or not, could ever have had beside them. Therefore, I am compelled to tell her story as she, and we have lived it. It's a story worth telling. This book is her eulogy and more.

One final point to ponder before closing and setting aside this book, give some thought to this particular fact—***they wear no uniform, no specific rank adorns their clothing, they are not promoted to any position beyond that which they currently have, earn no pay, nor achieve awards symbolized by medals, patches or ribbons; yet they contribute to the military service to which they have chosen to attach, just as much, and sometimes even more than their military person they married.*** We (Marines) simply refer to them as Marine Wife, but it could be Navy Wife, Army, Air Force, Coast Guard, or even Space Force Wife (spouse). It's an honored title. My Lyn lived it.

On 12 September, 2022, at 1320, my bride, my wife, my Lyn took her final breath. She died as I sat beside her. She had cancer and she fought until she could fight no more. She never complained, never assumed a "woe is me" posture, never felt bitter. And never gave up. I loved her more than life itself. I will miss her forever; however, most of all, I will remember and miss her stamina, her grit, her ability to adapt and overcome any and all obstacles except the very last one—the affliction of cancer. Forever—I will remember!

This book accurately reflects some of the more memorable portions of life and times we had together, the guidance she rendered, and more specifically—I will remember the almost unbelievable grace and dignity she displayed when overcoming the adversities in her, and our lives together. She certainly had more than her share of those; however, she always rose above the "sound and fury" most would exude while in those "valleys of despair." She was always the better person. She was my rock. She always demonstrated how strong people overcome life's adverse happenings. And, trust me, she was one hell of a strong person, all her life. She was my Semper Fi, my ***Marine Wife, Lyn***!

See you later, Baby!

. . .

POSTSCRIPT

This concept, or original thought for this book has an origin in a beautiful setting so appropriate for my late wife. That setting is holding an engraved brick, lining the winding pathway of the Semper Fidelis Memorial Park which overlooks the National Museum of the Marine Corps: On the visible surface of that brick, located with a multitude of similar bricks, it reads: *Major Ralph Stoney Bates USMC, (Ret)*. Those words etched into that brick, rest on a supporting foundation line. That supporting foundation, the last line, the bottom line inscribed into that same brick reads: *Marine Wife, Lyn.*

BRICK REGISTRATION CERTIFICATE

The

MARINE CORPS HERITAGE FOUNDATION

certifies this inscription

Major Ralph Stoney
Bates USMC, (Ret)
Marine Wife, Lyn

is to be engraved on a Brick lining the winding pathways of Semper Fidelis Memorial Park
overlooking the National Museum of the Marine Corps

LtGen Robert R. Blackman, Jr. USMC (Ret)
PRESIDENT & CEO
MARINE CORPS HERITAGE FOUNDATION

33673

Certificate

An array of remembrances, passports and photographs

EPILOGUE

It was very difficult to engage in writing a story of one's life, especially one I have loved and admired for over sixty-four years. I have, to the best of my abilities of recall, trust in God, and faith in my Marine Corps core principles, told it as it was. No embellishments, all factual events, good and bad. It was also difficult to tell my wife's life-story without injecting so much of my own life story into the story-line. It simply could not be avoided because our lives were and are forever intertwined, so much that removing one would tend to diminish the other. Therefore, the story has a tendency be a story of two people with emphasis on her. One would be incomplete without the other. The events are real. As best as I can remember, it's a truthful rendition of two lives, again with emphasis, as best I could portray, on my bride, ***Marine Wife, Lyn.***

In sticking to factual events, some remarks in the texts cast undesired, but not undeserved shadows over some characters and events in this story. I did not invent those shadows, nor did I name those characters. I presented them as unnamed people within events that occurred. To do otherwise, to omit altogether, would be not only inappropriate, it would also dismiss or diminish truths. Events happened and are told as I remember them, as nothing told was invented by me.

It is respectfully requested that profits from sales of this book go to the Marine Corps Heritage Foundation (90%) and to the Low Country Leathernecks

(10%) as long as they are actively engaged in promoting the memory of United States Marines and those who support them, in memory of my *Marine Wife, Lyn.*

Ralph Stoney Bates
Major USMC (Ret)
Mt. Pleasant, South Carolina

In Memory of Linda "Lyn" Gale Bates
21 February 1942-12 September 2022
My Marine Wife, Lyn

He that outlives a wife whom he has long loved, sees himself disjoined from the only mind that has the same hopes, and fears, and interest; from the only companion with whom he has shared much good and evil; and with whom he could set his mind at liberty, to retrace the past or anticipate the future. The continuity of being is lacerated; the settled course of sentiment and action is stopped; and life stands suspended and motionless.

Samuel Johnson
Born: September 18, 1709
Died: December 13, 1784 (aged 75)